GREAT DROPS OF BLOOD

BLOOD

THE GREATEST SALVATION

STORY EVER

Creative Ministry Resources Publishing Email: creativeministry_music@gmail.com

Paperback ISBN: 978-1-955809-46-7

Hardback ISBN: 978-1-955809-47-4

Ebook ISBN: 978-1-955809-48-1

INDEX

PREFACE

THE SALVATION STORY I TOLD:

ALMOST 100% POSITIVE RESPONSE

The sacrifice is ever understated
For it is very rarely ever understood
He was roughed up for you;
battered and crushed for you
But the mystery of the pain is the mastery of the cross
You will be surprised when you get the revelation
There is urgency for everyone who learns
The content of the pain, the extent of the pain,
Who actually bore the brunt of the pain
(Not just Jesus)
And the reason why we can no longer ignore or put Him off

The conflict of love captured in a tale
Is to witness passion in pursuit
And its expression filled with pain
Will spark a conflict of love in you.
It brings you into the game
With a passion to respond to Him,
and a passion for witnessing
(Not just to witness passion
but to witness with, and of, passion)
So love suffers not in vain

The sun had risen in the sky as I drove away from Bobby's workshop located in Mandeville, Jamaica. I had left Rhema and Halle-jah, my son and daughter there with him for music lessons. I was headed back to Saint Elizabeth, the adjoining parish on missions. Bobby was a family friend, a minister of the gospel and a music minister who operated a music school from his workshop. He trained church choirs, worship teams and individuals in a number of instruments and voices. The children anticipated this time as they were in the company of other children.

I prayed continuously as I headed down Spur Tree Hill, the longest hill in Jamaica. My mission would start anywhere in the parish. I had a heart for the parish. St. Elizabeth is known as the bread basket of the nation and the general income came from farming. My mission was to witness to as many persons within a three-hour time span and to return to collect the children by 2:00pm. I had made a covenant not to eat in St. Elizabeth for a year but to focus on its spiritual life. At times I would kneel in the squares or any other place and pray, symbolically pulling down strongholds and every high thing exalting itself against the knowledge of God.

Today was a very fruitful day. I had spoken to eighteen persons, some individually and some in groups and they all gave their lives to Christ. I had taken their names and numbers for follow up and to pray for them continuously.

I had very unusual success in the St. Elizabeth mission. Over 96% of the people I spoke with gave their hearts to Christ. This was somewhat a spoiler since 100% gave their lives in the first few weeks. It was only at the end that about three persons deferred.

What was unusual about my success was not my style or ability, but the message.

In this book, I will share the message I shared with these persons in long and short formats. This book is otherwise a detailed analogy of this message that takes the reader into the depths of truth hidden in the Biblical account of the event I am about to describe.

I believe you will be personally blessed and inspired by the revelation in this book. It will help you understand the reality beyond the pain of the cross. To tap into the real source of the pain and not be distracted by the drama of the physical through the excruciating reality of the cross.

This secret will motivate unbelievers to make this their moment and believers to be more deliberate with their Christian walk. It will motivate everyone to arm themselves and enter into battle to avenge the heart that fluttered for us until it was silenced and help everyone to be great witnesses.

INTRODUCTION

The fear of death none can describe
Knowing it is just a matter of time
Yet in no way can it compare
To anguish driven death from fear
But even worse than painful death
That tortures to the final breath
Agonizing trepidation; nothing above
The dread that turns the sweat to blood.

"Is it, is that…Ah!"

The building was shaking; concrete was falling; there was panic everywhere. He could hear the screams of his neighbors mixed into the blender of his own thoughts. A block of concrete fell on his leg. A piece of steel pierced his shoulders. He could not move. In that split second the blended panic had solidified into piercing agonizing pain. The pain was unbelievable even as the panic screamed at him with flashes of his life from childhood. He had no possibility of escape. Things were still crumbling all around him and with it his world. The smell of cement filled his nostrils. The dust filled his eyes and completely blocked visibility. It was a major earthquake. It was just a moment. Before he had time to accept how fragile his world really was, he heard it, a loud, frightening sound as if, as if... he did not have time to scream. The ceiling and walls came crashing, crumbling. He could feel himself become a part of the rubble of steel, concrete, human flesh, bones, blood, metal, paper, and wood. His last thoughts. It was over in forty-five seconds.

This is the reality of many earthquakes. The stories of the moment are left to the imagination of those who attempt to pull the bodies from the rubble, where they can be separated.

Yet history records a moment that did not involve death, or even physical pain but was even more punishing.

~~~~~~~~
~~~~~~~~

Bang! The sound was unbelievably loud, but it was momentary. He was lost in a moment of disbelief filled with intense pain. He was swimming in his own blood. Glass and metal were stuck in his body. He caught a glimpse of the trailer truck on top of his car. The blood was filling his lungs. Then he saw the fire. The pain was intense. There was no time. The lights were going…

His ordeal lasted two minutes. He had time to embrace death. It was something he was never prepared for. He had time to make peace with himself before the intense fire numbed him to pain and took him out completely.

This was intense but nothing close to the moment that forms the focus of this book.

~~~~~~~~~

He saw the blood in the water and wondered where it came from. The pain hit him in that moment but he had no time to process it, something was pulling him under the water…
~~~~~~~~~

This too reflects the experience of many who died painful premature deaths. His mind exploded in an anguished scream that was muted and cut short as his head submerged. He held his breath and screamed internally as he kicked with all his might. Then he felt it. An unbelievable pain as teeth sunk deeper into his flesh. He briefly caught the eyes of the crocodile before the roll began. It shook every attempt to control his breathing. He gasped for breath and swallowed what seemed like a gallon of water. It was all he had time to remember.

This is a terrible death but is still nothing close to the agony we are about to describe.

~~~~~~~~~~~~~

The stories above are some real life situations that describe some of the painful sudden deaths that take place in our world every day. These deaths by accidents, war or crime are the most common causes of untimely deaths that are intense but normally momentary.

Painful deaths are however emphasized when they are prolonged. There are people who have lived with
~~~~~~~~~~~~~

physical pain for days and years and with sicknesses which eventually take their lives. Many have suffered from cancer and other conditions so painful that their loved ones are happy for them when death ends the suffering.

Death is a reality. Unexpected death should not be embraced yet it should be anticipated. It should not be prepared for but prepared against. In other words, preparedness is a state not a statement or an event.

The experience of Jesus surpassed all these spoken of. He sweated blood in anticipation of His death, yet He did not die from fear. He had to face the fear that caused His anguish. He died while experiencing the agonizing reality and painful experience of the moment He dreaded.

~~~~~~~~~

Jesus says, "No man knows the hour…" Of a rich man who had no sense of his spiritual reality and who chose to build barns instead of pursuing a relationship with God, "Today your soul is required of you."
~~~~~~~~~

James 4 says, life is like a vapor; don't say tomorrow I will go there or do this, rather say, if the Lord wills...

Death occurs in many packages often mixed with unbearable pain. Some persons have been beaten to death, some stoned, some mauled, some frozen, some crashed from the sky, some suffocated, some drowned, and many other painful, horrible and frightful ways.

The death we are about to describe surpasses them all. It is a unique moment in history where a certain person anticipating his death, experienced more pain than the excruciation of the moment could ever have caused, more pain than history will ever repeat. His name is Jesus.

Luke 22 verse 44: "He was in so much pain, anguish, agony and extreme torment mentally that His sweat was as it were great drops of blood falling to the ground."

In the book we seek to determine the truth about His mental anguish. Was it the fear of the pain of death? Certainly He was not the only one who anticipated extreme torture and painful death. Many after Him suffered painful deaths and torture in life in His name.

They faced it with bravery, confidence and joy by thinking of Him. It cannot be that His followers are braver than Him, their inspiration. If not, then why did He sweat blood the way He did?

~~~~~~~~

Peter was in prison. His fate was prophesied by his Master. He was told that he would live until he is old, then people would carry him where he did not want to go. The council had condemned him. He knew they had determined to crucify him. He said boldly, "I am not worthy to be crucified as my Master, crucify me upside down."

They obliged.

~~~~~~~~

The missionary was in prison. He was considered a political prisoner with an enemy that did not recognize rules. The Muslims had banned proselyting. He was always threading in dangerous territory. He was betrayed and captured. They were brutal. He overheard the soldier responsible for his torture discussing with an army general ways to make his torture as painful as possible. He knew they meant it. He could hear the screams of others being tortured throughout the day, every day for the three days he was there. Their screams were a part of his torture. He knew some of them. Some were his converts. Some screamed and rebelled, yet some died with such peace calling on the name of the Lord.

He could overhear a Muslim prisoner say, "This Jesus, whoever He is, has inspired such confidence in death in His followers. He must have been a very brave person Himself. Unafraid of death and challenges. Well, I am not. I can't sleep."

The missionary looked over at him. He was sweating and trembling. The anticipation of death was so punishing for him. He was not a Christian. He loved his life and the discussion about torture would set off a chain of reaction that would give him sleepless nights. He had nightmares and no comfort. Time ticked and his body screamed from within…

The missionary was calm. He went over to him and said, "Can I tell you about Jesus?"

What did he tell him? Did he tell him the story of this brave untroubled Jesus who went to His death without concern or even fear of the moment? Did he tell him about the garden of Gethsemane? Certainly, that would not have brought comfort in the moment. Yet he did and the Muslim gave his life. He had peace facing his own demise. He no longer trembled. He was no longer frightened. So what did he tell him about a Master who sweated blood facing His own death that could have given him such peace?

The mystery unfolds in this book.

~~~~~~~

They say nothing beats a moment's reality than the moment you know it: you know what is coming, you know the intensity of what is coming and you have to live through it in the moments leading up to it. The moments you not only tough it out but you sweat it out. Yet, it has never been heard that any person agonized so much that their sweat became, as it were, great drops of blood.

Yet for Jesus it happened.
~~~~~~~

This moment is what we are about to dissect and it is guaranteed to inspire you to appreciate the love of God so much more.

BOOK I

CONFLICTS OF THE CROSS

PAIN: THE UNCONVENTIONAL MIXING MACHINE

History is known for this
The emotions disarray that pain will mix
Make hormones flow and pressure range
When anxiety rides on the setting rain
But never had it been spoken of
Pain and agony's boiling pot
Not mental just, but physical reach
Where vessels burst and mixture breach
No physical wound; no, never seen
Such an unconventional pain-mixing
machine

The producer was busy preparing the setting for the most iconic and important scene history would ever shoot. Much though had gone into planning. "Should I choose the temple? Perhaps no. Too religious and common a setting. He would be easily identifiable and would be in the arms of His enemies. They must come for Him. The betrayer must have His day. A desert, that would certainly allow for seclusion? No, must be easily accessible and a place one would resort to for rest and relaxation. A garden? Perfect! Must be a garden that is not used all the time. Must be large enough to allow individuals to have their own space. Must be empty for this scene. He can be over there. Perfect! His three lieutenants can be… over there; perfect! Some distance away. He will need personal time.

Ready, set, go!

No, this was not a created scene; it was real life. This was no play acting. Could it be…? The blood that mixed with His sweat looked like a scene out of movie but… but this was no acting. This was too real. This was a moment the mystery of the science of the human body was being redefined by pain. Never has it been heard before that human sweat turned to blood and never again would it be. This is no scene the producer could have produced. This is something science cannot explain. This is something worthy of investigation and analysis. The deep mysteries of the moment are about to be unveiled in this book.

~~~~~~~~

The setting was a scenic and somewhat isolated garden. It was a place that connected the heart with the silent yet audible serenading melody of nature. It made a perfect place for a quiet retreat and prayer. This person had made it a personal prayer retreat for Himself and His mentees.

Today would be so different. He was here with His three lieutenants. This place which would have brought solace could not free Him from the burden He bore. It could not bring relief from the excruciation of the pain that tore through His heart and soul. This pain was the most severe He had ever experienced, yet it was anticipatory rather than active; it was premeditation rather than present. It was about something that was about to happen that mesmerized Him. By revelation, He was fully aware of the intimate details of every moment of it.
~~~~~~~~

His reaction was natural, yet this pain was not natural; it plummeted beyond mental anguish to a spiritual rupture that the human senses could not describe or absorb. It was louder than His blood vessels could contain and more piercing than His sweat glands could resist. His sweat could not resist the drumming of the blood vessels. It surrendered and allowed them entry. They immediately took control and turned His sweat to great drops of blood. It was a mixture created by extremely painful emotional distress. Yet this was all sheer anticipatory pain.

Indeed, the moment is a picture of mental anguish and torture with intensity to the highest power. It is the reality of something that was actually taking place based on the realization of something that was about to take place; something difficult, something unbearable, something painful, yet not something immediate but something imminent.

~~~~~~~
~~~~~~~

He was kneeling there in silence with no desire or passion for sleep. If sleep was to venture near, the mental distress would scare it way.

This was what appeared to be Jesus' weakest moment yet it would inspire such great strength in His followers.

He turned His anguish to prayer. His prayer was agonizing because His prayer found its rest in His destiny and His destiny sapped the energy from His prayer.

The target of His prayer was the object of His pain and His resignation to the moment.

If you understand this parable you will understand His agony but you don't have to agonize to understand it, it will be explained in detail in this book.

The energy with which He prayed and the energy with which He agonized caused Him to sweat and not just to sweat ordinarily but to sweat profusely. The struggle that was taking place inside Him almost had the effect of a literal fight. Although it was a fight internally, it was a fight with Himself and with His destiny. It caused blood to be shed. His blood vessels burst in His sweat glands with such proportion they poured into the sweat that was on His body. His sweat was so profuse that it dropped from Him like great drops, like rain drops. In those drops were the blood and the blood was red. That was an agonizing moment like few have ever encountered. It is very hard to imagine.

The question is why would this great inspirer of confidence and assurance sweat so much because of anticipation of what was to come? Was He afraid of death, the same death His followers face so boldly?

Many of this Man's followers would die in very agonizing ways: some at the stake, burnt, Peter who was fast asleep, would be crucified upside down, some pelted with stones, some by physical and mental torture, abused in every way, bodies torn apart, yet they still held firm with their confidence and their joy even intensified. Peter and John would be whipped maliciously with flesh-tearing power yet they would rejoice that they were counted worthy to suffer shame for this Man. This Man who seems to not just be ordinarily fearful about the death He was about to face, but extraordinarily fearful, so much that He sweated blood.

Why would the Son of God agonize so much about something that was easily His destiny? Why would it cause Him so much pain and cause this level of reaction within His body? Could it be the suffering He would suffer on the cross? And indeed He suffered. Could it be the rejection He would face? Could it be the nails that pierced His hand? Why, why?

Was it the death or was it the depth, that went beyond the death and the suffering to something else? What could that something else be that inspired this blood-sweating moment?

Is there more to this moment than meets the eye?

~~~~~~~~~~

The target of His prayer was the object of His pain and His resignation to the moment. He had no help from the heavens.
~~~~~~~~~~

Again if you understand this parable you will understand His agony but you don't have to agonize to understand it, it will be explained.

We are about to take you on a journey that will expose more than the moment but expose you in this moment to that something, or perhaps, that something else.

This cannot be dated because it predated time. The journey was completed although it was not fully executed in time. This Person had already finished the journey although He was in the garden, still moments before the journey would capture Him and suck Him into its macabre depths. He was in the center of the moment, the most painful heart-rending reality of it… and He struggled. Ah! He never knew He would struggle like this. He never knew love could pain this much.

The journey started in eternity where a human sacrifice was made of God, which is another parable. We now take you there.

The reality of knowing
When you are living in the skies
That your destiny is showing
You must the brought down from on high
Streets of gold and angel worship
To face the man whom you create
To be spit on and rejected
And put in the lowest place

To wear dirt for a clothing
And to be treated just the same
Yet all the time you are holding
Glory swallowed up in shame

The refulgence of the Father and the Son filled the atmosphere with radiant splendor. Its incandescence reached every part of the third heavens with such a warmth and splendorous aura that it could be felt. It brought such a feeling of rest, wellbeing and of joy to the fullness. It was not just called glow it was called glory.

Not only was the Son jointly the light of glory that billions of angels basked in, but there was such an appreciation of the presence, an appreciation of the Person, an appreciation of the glow that filled every being inside and out. It inspired worship constantly.

They bowed down before this being and lovingly and reverentially crooned, "Holy, holy; holy, holy, holy."

They did this continually because there was no night. The light was the light of the Father and Son and the light inspired worship. Worship never stopped because His presence carried the glow that made it glory. The recognition of glory is worship.

They ascribed to Him worth, lauding His splendor, His wisdom, His power, His riches, His honor and His creation of all things visible and invisible.

Such was His position, highly exalted.

Well, we have spoken about His position, let us speak about the place. The place is beyond anything this earth can imagine. It is the highest place ever created. It is the place where the Creator of all things lives so you can imagine its grandeur. In fact, all creation borrows from its glory and is simply a reflection of it.

In all other places, riches and wealth is defined by measurement, but this place where riches cannot be measured defines riches and wealth. In all other places, streets are made of stones but there, streets are made of gold. A picture of that place makes us understand that everything the earth has is borrowed. The colors here are borrowed there they are brilliant, and perfect. The waters here are borrowed because even the best of our waters cannot be compared to the crystal living waters that flow from the throne there. The gold on earth is borrowed because the gold there is as clear as glass. Angels here are borrowed because that is the place angels live.

Can you imagine anyone leaving there to come and take residence here and even so in a position that would befit a slave?

It was in that place the Son, who was one with the Father, who could feel the Father's heart, who knew the

Father's thoughts, who at all times had the same heart, thoughts and mind of the Father, was pained similarly with Him by their creation, earth.

The earth was not just a normal place. It was a place God loves dearly. It was filled with a specie that God made deliberately in His image and whom He had great expectations of. God placed everything in the earth to sustain life unlike the other planets He created. Everything was created for this special specie. He created other living things by speaking, but for Him, speaking would not suffice for this specie, though it would have worked. He wanted to place Himself inside this specie and the only way to do so was to get personal. He came down and got personally engaged in intricate molding with His hands while His thought of love, which one author stated was more than the sand by the sea, kept running. He took His time with the curves and shape until He perfected it. Then He kissed it with His own breath.

After all this process, it is just natural that heaven was emotionally and spiritually tied to the creature. The creature He created is called man.

The Devil, another of His creation, had corrupted a third of the angels in heaven and was cast down to earth. He saw this as a perfect opportunity to corrupt and steal the work of God and he was successful. Man was living in rebellion against God. They began sinning against God doing everything contrary to the heart of God and the instructions that He had for them. He had no option but to destroy them… well unless…

Yes, we spoke about it, the Prince of glory would have to take on the role of a commoner, a slave, for by His own decree, only a man could intervene in this place, earth, where man lived.

This was a paradox, an extreme conflict. It was a choice between love and love; the love of the word and the love of His Son. It would mean that God had to sacrifice Someone whom He loved dearly in heaven; in so doing He was sacrificing Himself. The Father, the Son and the Holy Spirit settled on the conclusion. It is documented in the human Bible in John 3:16. It states how love would inspire God to give His Son, His only begotten Son. Love would compel Him to give His Son. Love would demand of Him His Son and He would respond by giving in to love. Love would cause a division in heaven that was even greater than the division that caused the devil himself to be cast out, a division we are about to define.

Stepping away from Glory would be a significant sacrifice for the Son. It was all about what He was stepping away from, or rather out of, or should we say, out of and away from and what He was stepping into, or should we say, what was about to step into Him. It is all about the covering, the clothing and the treatment. Yet the treatment of the place did not change His glory or His grace, but in either place, His treatment would be completely different. When the value of something is not recognized it is often abused. In this new place, His value was disguised by His clothing of clay. He had to step down from eternity and step away from His glory and His very nature. He had to allow the Father to shine alone in heaven while He came down to earth and become the light of this world. Though His throne is in Heaven and He is clothed in glory, love always gets down to earth.

He had the power to deliver man from Satan. He had the same power that cast him and his angels out. Is it that He could step down and use His mighty power to deliver man from sin and then step back up into glory? No; this was to be much more delicate. Is this why His sweat became as great drops of blood?

The answer to this question is found in the realization of a number of conflicts that culminated in one conflict that shook the earth and shook time. Was any or all of these conflicts responsible for the blood staging this dramatic escape from its blood vessels and pouring into His sweat?

So what are the conflicts the Son would face in becoming the savior of the world? We examine these conflicts.

Conflict #2 – DIVINELY HUMAN OR HUMAN DIVINE

Lost His divinity
Took on humanity
It was a moment in time the Word became flesh
Stepped out of Glory
Into our story
No one gives up the greater for less
The greatest of meekness
Subject to weakness
Flesh plagued with sin He would have to contend
Trapped in this body
Yet so pure and so holy
He condescended to this, God's will to attend

The first conflict the Son of God was to face was that of releasing His divinity and embracing humanity. If one could let go but still hold one; to gain the full benefits without paying the full price, many would. Jesus has no taste for this; He spits it out. For Him, there would be no divinely human or human divine. He would have to let go totally and become completely human.

Romans 8:3 explains this conflict. It says, "For what the law was powerless to do for it was weak because of the flesh, God sent His own Son packaged as sinful flesh so He could condemn sin in the flesh."

John 1:14 says: "The word became flesh and lived among us, and we saw His glory…"

The bite of this first conflict is that the flesh He was supposed to clothe Himself in was not pure but sinful. The privilege of the flesh is that He could operate like a normal man in the earth. Spirits have no authority here; they need flesh to function. Jesus did not come as spirit but as flesh which gave Him all the rights of dominion given to mankind. This automatically elevated

Him above the devil and His demons here. The disadvantage of wearing the flesh is that in the flesh He would suffer temptation just like any normal man, any human being. In the flesh, He was subject to sin just like any human being. In the flesh, He would have to resist sin the way a human being resisted. In the flesh, He exposed Himself to all the traps and the weaknesses of a normal human being. In the flesh, He did not have the protection of His divinity. In the flesh, He did not have the ability of His Father to mediate His own personal choices, He would have to exercise restraint. In the flesh, He had limited access to the angels that He had full command of in glory. In the flesh, He did not have this entourage of spiritual beings visibly present constantly as He had in heaven. In the flesh He would walk in the way of man, live in the way of man and be ordinary until He was separated unto His mission. He would engage the profession of man, doing the trade of His earthly father who was a carpenter. He would leave the place where heavenly beings are subjected to Him and would come to a place where He Himself would have to be subject to earthly beings… to His father, to His mother, to authority, to elders, to systems, rules and regulations. It was a far measure from the place where all authority and systems were subject to Him.

Indeed, in the flesh, Jesus was called to make Himself subject to His creation so He could redeem His creation. Is this why His sweat became as great drops of blood? Of course not, He passed all these hurdles before He came to that place in the Garden of Gethsemane. He passed all these hurdles before He stepped down out of Himself, out of eternity into time and took on the form of a human baby. He passed all these hurdles without a second thought. He was even slain already before He arrived.

But then, He was in agony. He agonized over a hurdle He was still yet to face. What was that conflict?

Could it be the conflict of man?

Conflict #3 THE CONFLICT OF MAN

Love has found its way
In your world what do you say?
Amen; amen!
Or do you chase it away
Disrespect it and refuse
Its arms extended
Hurting through the years
Love is seeking you with tears
You violently resist
What kind of love is this?

But it's must worse
When you treat it like a curse
Yet all you are is what it made you
The life you have; the life it gave you
So much worse
When you hate vehemently
The same One who gave to you the breath
of air

Will you please understand
This is: the conflict of man!

When Jesus made that decision to step out of eternity into time so He could redeem mankind from the corruption that had entered time and had entered man, He knew He would face the conflict of man. Hebrews 12:3 says, "Consider Him who endured such hostility from sinners against Himself."

He knew they would call Him names for doing good: for healing, for teaching, for demonstrating the kingdom of God. They called Him Beelzebub. They bedeviled Him and called Him the devil yet He had to endure this even though angels called Him holy, worthy, glorious, and exalted. He was to enter earth to defeat the devil and destroy his works on their behalf, but they would look at all His good and call Him Satan. He knew that was a conflict He would have to face.

He knew they would attempt to kill Him many times just for telling them the truth. Once He told them, "I and My Father are one."

They led Him to the brow of a hill and tried to cast Him down so His bones would be broken and He would die, but He passed through them and went on His way.

Their intent against Him and against what He was bringing would be murderous and He knew it. He would have to step out of His glory where He was celebrated just to give Himself for humanity who would not even appreciate Him. It is a conflict He would have to face. His own mother and brothers would try to stop His mission. They would call Him "mad", "loco", "out of Your mind" and they would seek to physically restrain Him to the point where He would have to deny the spirit in them. They would tell Him, "Go up to the feast if You want to be known" because they did not believe in Him. He would face the conflict of His own family members.

He was King living as a peasant in human world, totally disguised as ordinary flesh with an ordinary life but an extraordinary mission. This was a cause He gave Himself? Yet he knew He would be maltreated by the ones who needed Him most. Was this maltreatment justification to step away from Glory and embrace shame to save humankind? He knew this was a conflict He would have to face. His creation would spit in His face, buffet Him; mock Him, ridicule Him. It was a lot to think about but that could never fill His cup so as to cause His blood to panic and burst their restraining vessels.

His Father looked at Him then. Knowing everything that was in His Father's heart, (they were one), He had no hesitation. These conflicts were never a second thought.

Yet one gnawed at Him throughout. It would play out in the Garden of Gethsemane.

He bowed His head and conceded for there was something that He knew: the thing that causes man to behave the way they behaved is not that they were created bad but they were corrupted good. He knew that unless He dealt with the bad that had corrupted them and was corrupting them, the devil, the man would be completely lost. These creatures who had the potential to carry God and walk as gods would be Satan's dummies forever. These life-carrying beings would be walking dead.

He would go down to deal with the devil so that man would have the opportunity once more to live the life of gods. He had to become the sacrifice. He had to suffer all these things that He would face to redeem man.

The Bible tells us for this cause and purpose the Son of man was manifested that He may destroy the works of the devil. Unless the works of the devil were destroyed then man would remain in bondage.

And so He came and He faced all these conflicts. He worked tirelessly to redeem man. There was yet a major conflict to face, conflict number three.

Conflict #4 PLACING DIVINITY ON THE LINE TO BE LOST FOREVER

When you step out of character
You step into a place
Where you risk being caught out
Never to find it back again
Some would live in their fortress
Just to play it safe
But without the risk; without the hazard
There can be no real gain

The greatest risk of humanity
When you place divinity on the line
Is to let it go to reach others
Who may treat eternity as time

Certainly, a major conflict that Jesus must have faced was the conflict of His divinity. John would record, "The Word became flesh and dwelt among us and we beheld His glory."

Some may argue that He exposed His divinity, but He not only exposed His divinity, He surrendered it. The major conflict is that the moment Jesus became flesh He faced the conflict of losing His divinity forever. Jesus knew this very well. Satan knew this also. As a human He would be tempted in all points as every human being. It is recorded that He would be without sin, but have you considered; what would have happened to His divinity if He had sinned?

While Jesus was in heaven He was above principalities and powers. He could not be tempted. In fact, a law was written about Him, "You shall not temp the Lord Your God."

He knew that the moment He clothed Himself in flesh He relinquished that right. He would live in a place where the devil taught men to ignore the word and tested them to see if they knew the word. Here He would be subject to all the temptation of man. If He was to ever concede to any of these temptations, He would lose His divinity forever.

By coming to die for man, He was placing His divinity on the line for humanity. He was doing this for human beings who had stepped away from the Presence of God and fallen into the trap of sin.

<p style="text-align:center">~~~~~~~</p>

The atmosphere was dry and humid. The cracked earth lifted its voice and cried to the clouds dancing above. The cloud was lost in its own world and gave no indication that it heard the cry of the earth below. The soil lifted its hands begging the clouds to change its beautiful blue garment to black. That just momentarily it would take on the garment of mourning and shed tears so that the earth could catch a little. It refused, and continued its tireless dance. The earth mouthed a strong argument, "Send it to me and I will send the water back to you in evaporation."

The clouds ignored her.

A young man mopped the sweat from his brow as he journeyed with his wife and infant son. He was married through controversial circumstances and had recently delivered his firstborn. His child had become an immediate target of the devil. He had incited the heart of the king, and so this young man, was running away. His destination was Egypt.

With Jesus coming to earth, He had become a target of the devil immediately. The devil wanted His life and His destiny. Joseph was warned and sent to Egypt to escape. Herod was so furious and so intentional that He committed infanticide against all male children under two years old.

With the devil on the loose and in command, the coming of Jesus to earth in the form of man would be treacherous. It would not take the devil long to strike. Throughout His youth, Jesus would be tempted in every way man is tempted but after He was baptized, His mission was attacked by Satan Himself.

The Spirit compelled Him to fast in the wilderness. The Bible says He drove Him to the wilderness. It was a pre-emptive fast. A time of significant testing was imminent. The burden was so severe that He fasted for forty days and forty nights. It was then that the devil came.

He came to Jesus, starved of food but He was full of the word and the spirit. The devil tempted Him in all areas of temptation, the lust of the flesh, the lust of the eyes and pride. Jesus overcame by word precision and the devil departed for a season, it was not finished.

If Jesus had given in to any of these temptations, heaven would be permanently closed to Him. He would no longer be the Son of God. He would be a rebel just like the devil himself. He would have submitted Himself to a new father. He would have lost His divinity. He placed His divinity on the line for humanity. He knew He would have to do this but this did not bother Him.

Of course this could not have been the cause of the great drops of blood. The moment in the Garden of Gethsemane was after He faced and conquered all these tests. Something else must have inspired this passionate moment. Something much worse. Something not yet faced, not yet conquered, but sitting on the horizon like an ominous monster.

BOOK 2

THE ROAD AHEAD

Could it be the pain of His great agony
That made His sweat turn blood
     Was much more than what He'd faced and conquered
But all about what was yet to come?
Yet could it be both are connected
And the source of this great pain
Was in the past that lay before Him
The present, which is, and was before He came?

He was thirty-three years of age. For most of His life, the first thirty years, He lived a normal life with His mother, siblings and His father who had died. He was a man anointed by the Holy Spirit. Acts 10:38 demystifies the God He was, says nothing about God in Him and instead magnifies the God on Him, the Holy Spirit. The last three years of His life He ministered by the Holy Spirit. That same Spirit that descended on Him empowering Him is the same

Spirit living in those who believe Him, empowering them in the same way He was empowered.

For the three years of His ministry, He worked tirelessly. He once told someone who said, "I will follow You wherever You go," that "the foxes have holes and the birds have nests but the Son of man has no place to lay His head". Such was His tireless effort. He walked from town to town and multitudes followed Him. There were times He had no food, the disciples were hungry once and plucked corn from the stalk in the field and ate it raw. He faced the element of nature, strong storms, yet the worst of all the storms He would face is the storm of people. The storms of those who He came to save, who objected to Him, who contested with Him, who fought against Him and who would eventually kill Him.

Here He was, knowing that His time was short and among His faithful disciples was a betrayer. The storm with the strongest wind created by those closest to you. Jesus came to the garden knowing He knew He would be betrayed by the same people He came to save. He could feel the wind of those who would betray Him, those who would deny Him, those who would celebrate His demise, those who would mock Him, those who would whip Him, those who would spit on Him…storms. Here He was, all these were His past, He encountered them and He conquered them although they were yet to manifest.

There was something ahead of Him that was causing Him great pain. As He stood there in the Garden of Gethsemane the thought caused Him to agonize in prayer. It was too much for Him to carry. He prayed with passion and kept praying. The intensity was so much that He sweated so much that the sweat began to drop like rain. Not only did He sweat salted water, the color was crimson. The blood vessels had burst in His sweat glands because of the concentration and energy He exerted as He prayed distressed. It was not just a soft mixture that could go unnoticed. It was not just a trace of brown when the face was wiped. His sweat became great drops of blood. It was apparent.

So why did His sweat become as great drops of blood? Was it something He had already encountered or something He was about to face? Could it be something He had already encountered and that He was yet about to face, perhaps, just as He was slain in the past but not yet in the present. Could it be something He had not overcome but He understood? Something He had not engaged but now He could not ignore because the past was imminent (pardon the confusion), and the future was present.

Could it be... could it be the intensity of His pain was still ahead of Him? Could it be... could it be that His present reality was more than the physical sacrifice in His near future? We search for answers in this volume.

THE ANGUISH OF BETRAYAL

As He knelt down to pray in the Garden of Gethsemane, by the revelation of the Holy Spirit, He was not spared the gruesome details of His approaching demise. He could see it unfold prophetically in 6D. It all began within minutes from that moment. He thought on His disciples, betraying Him, forsaking Him, denying Him. He could see Judas:

Friend, you walked with Me,
Three years you've talked with Me
All I had you shared with Me
Now…friend!
Yes, you would share your heart with Me
All this time you found not fault in Me
You shared sweats and laughs with Me
Is thirty pieces what all that this was worth?

Take it back it feels so dirty
Take it back it was a lie
Take it back, it brings me misery

I have come to realize
Money cannot purchase or replace
The joy I had with Christ
O how I wish that I could take back…
Friend…He called me…
Tears were running from his eyes

He knew that all his disciples would soon depart from Him, every one of them. He could see…rather he could hear their rowdiness; the soldiers meant business.

"Get Him!" they shouted. It was a squad of soldiers, boisterous and very aggressive. They were rough and they were intentional. Leading them was someone He loved dearly; someone who was with Him daily; who ate at His table, fed from His love; one of His disciples. This was someone who was among the twelve closest to Him and who went everywhere He went. It was someone Jesus entrusted with the finances of His group… not that He placed confidence in that moneybag anyway; He knew the wealth He carried. This person had placed too much confidence in the moneybag. He was given it to carry but instead, it carried him… yes, even to his own destruction.

This rogue disciple's job was to set up the moment of His capture. He had inside information about where Jesus would be. Jesus saw him coming to Him in a disarming manner contrasting with the soldiers behind him. He reached out as if for a friend. Jesus saw his hands but was placing careful attention to his heart which He could see more clearly. There was such a contradiction it was tangible. The smile on his face was so warm and welcoming it deceitfully contrasted the armed and angry soldiers he led. The kiss He extended sent a strong electrical shockwave into the Lord's body. It was generated by the contrast of the wickedness of His heart and the friendly gesture he displayed. In the realm of the man it is called hypocrisy and betrayal. He came in and landed the kiss and Jesus permitted him. He accepted it for the many who would be betrayed in life by individuals who would get this close… as close as the cheek, but who unlike Him, could not taste the heart of the one kissing them. Judas heard Jesus say, "Friend!" It completely disarmed him.

No this is not the past; it was the immediate future, just moments away, but it was a part of a very bitter package. His response in the minute showed the small impact this would have on Him. It was easy for Him to forgive. The sweat of blood… no! It could not attract this measure of reaction.

His statement in the moment, "friend!" was a statement of relationship that summarized betrayal. It was a statement of where His heart was and how distant the other person's heart was from His. It was a statement of intention, of potential that was lost in a moment of bad decision and in a moment of greed. It was a statement of eternity that was being denied in a moment of flesh. "Friend, do you betray the Son of man with a kiss?"

He saw Peter coming. He was very angry. He had a sword and passionately wanted to defend his Master. Peter was very passionate and impulsive. He took the sword and struck a soldier and his ear flew off. Jesus knew how divisive that moment could have been for Peter. To disarm the moment Jesus took that ear and placed it back on as He counseled Peter.

The soldiers grabbed Him roughly and treated Him like a common criminal. No one had ever treated Him like that before. He could see it and feel it all as He prayed to the Father. He saw them grab Him and push Him. It was hurting Him. They treated Him as if He was nobody, as if He was some trash to be taken out. Yet the kiss of Judas was even more stunning, even more painful. It left Him feeling… dirty, low, belittled, very hurt, but, this did not even cause Him to sweat as He prayed. All these were human feelings. It was something else; something more severe; something more traumatic.

DENIED; FORSAKEN; LEFT TO BEAR HIS PAIN ALONE

In the moment reflection, or should I say, anticipation, as He prayed, He could see them, all His disciples, all His followers, everyone, forsaking Him, running away, fleeing. The one He loved, the one who leaned on His arm, the one who said he would never desert Him; he would follow Him wherever He went. The one who said let us go with Him so we may die with Him; and the one... in fact, all the other ones. They all forsook Him and ran away. He was alone, alone with the soldiers being shoved and pushed around.

The thought came as a sharp pain to His heart where He kept them all; it was a special place for His disciples. It left as quickly as it came. It absconded in the conquering thought, "Of all you have given me I have lost none."

I swear I do not know Him

Never seen this Man before

Could I not have remained quiet

And let silence be my words
Wisdom would have applauded
And everyone would hear
And my heart would not rebuke me
Nor my river brim with tears

He heard the rooster crowing
As he told that final lie
His heart sunk like a casket
As he caught his Master's eye
It was the love and the forgiveness
It was the best friend he denied
It was the tears that fell like rain drops
And the misery when it dried.

He could see Peter in the distance following. He could see John using his influence to get into the hall and opening the door to Peter. None of the two presented themselves as His disciple or even as an associate. Peter vehemently denied he knew Him. It was painful. He did not want to be recognized; he did not want to be identified with this person who was being condemned. This person; the person he followed so extravagantly with all his impulsiveness, he now denied so vehemently.

Jesus sighed. Extremely painful!

He saw Himself making eye contact with Peter then, convicting but not condemning, instead reassuring him. That was for Peter but there was no one to soothe the pain running havoc in His own heart. The other disciples were nowhere to be seen, nowhere to be found. They were hiding, they were afraid. He remembered that He had said to Peter that the devil had asked to sift him like wheat; that he would be strengthened and a source of strength to the others. He had already prayed for Peter. He had overcome this also. It did not factor in His sweat and certainly not in the agony that compelled His vessels to secrete blood.

Well could it be a combination, or should I say, a compilation of all these factors? Those were emotional moments to face; very severe emotional punishment combined with extreme physical agony. Could the rejection of His friends; yes, friends, added to the aggression of His enemies, added to the affliction of His body, have caused His blood to defy science and pour into His sweat glands?

No! These were all human occurrences. They did not trigger the intensity of His pain He felt as He prayed. Yes, they were painful but they were human pain. Many would go through the same in various forms. If these did not trigger the intensity of His mental anguish, what then?

THE WHIPPING POST

It was feared by many
A heartless boast
The fury of the whipping post
The torturer's strength would come to bear
The blood would spill as flesh would tear
The iron tips would touch the bone
At least they'd try and when they're done
The pain would last for many days
The sweat of blood did this create?

So if it was not His disciples then what could it be? Was it the pain that He was supposed to suffer on the cross? Was it the rejection? Was it the atrocious spanking? Was it the excruciation of emotional chaos and physical havoc combined? In fact, that is the most obvious explanation and the most obvious cause, but, what was it?

He could hear the grunt of the man handling the whip. Everything else was silent. Even the insects were cooperating, fearing to give their position away in this terrifying moment. Then He heard the distinct sound of the whip sailing through the air with a whistle as it mustered its most ferocious speed to attack the back of a monstrous enemy. Then His back bent in impact and a groan of severe pain involuntarily escaped His lips. He was the enemy; the whip was never instructed about His innocence. The barbarous soldiers jeered. It happened again and again until the pain swallowed up His count. His back simply sagged and surrendered to its torment. It did not stiffen in anticipation anymore. When they were finished, He had to be carried away to recover.

As He prayed in the garden He could see it all prophetically. He was kneeling there, the clothes stripped from His body. He could hear in His ear the anger of the man carrying the whip. He was big and strong, looking just like a body builder. He could see the grimace on his face as he menacingly lifted up the whip with those metal tips. He could see the bare muscles as he powered down with all his strength on His back. As he dragged it out the flesh parted and the blood spew as if from a ruptured pipe. He could see and feel it all. It was more than enough to make anyone break in pain.

The thought was mental torture as He prayed. It did not move Him. He prayed on beyond this flash point without flinching. No, this did not cause His sweat to become blood but it incited its own human reaction.

REJECTION OF THE JEWS

Pain borne alone keeps bearing down
Where no help or comfort to be found
And Satan persist; there was no slack
His innocence clear but matters not
Where condemnation and rejection fused
Where words of hate become abuse
And judgment comes with the judge
confused
No guilt or fault; my judgment set
The hammer sound; condemned to death.

This moment was no poetry it was pure pain, though the poets would put the moment to passionate songs later.

He could hear them. He looked into the faces of the many whom He had healed. Some of the same who had come and lifted their voices while He rode into Jerusalem successfully saying, "Hosanna! Hosanna in the highest! Blessed is He who comes in the name of the

Lord!" Now some of those same voices were crying vehemently, "Crucify Him! Crucify Him!"

Painful! Very painful!

He could see the hate on the faces of some of those He had healed, whose parents He had delivered, whose families He had touched, whom He had fed, whom He had led; whom He had comforted. This was His weakest moment in the flesh; He was being crucified; He was being tormented; He was condemned to death and… yes, distinctly, He could hear the voices that lauded Him, mocking Him. In the weakness of His human flesh it was a muffled fusion of noise, insults, personal injury competing with the pain, shame and heartbreak; each seeking prominence; yet each having its own tortuous effect. None of His senses was acute enough in that moment to separate one from the other so the moment passed in a muffled echo of shame, pain and personal injury mixed together to become a strong poisonous fume that stifled the very air of oxygen and caused wave after wave of electric shocks through His frail body.

The soldiers, spat in His face, hit Him as if He was nothing and buffeted Him as they laughed and joked about it. He could feel the pain of their rejection. The same persons who fought to make Him King were now the loudest in this rowdy crowd, all wanting to see His shameful death. It was painful; very painful!

Emotionally drained; physically drained, He could feel it all though His heart refused to process anything but love. In times like these, you focus on whatever thing is good, pure, just, lovely and of good report. Everything else would have made Him equal with the ones executing wickedness against Him; would lower Him to their level. He could feel the pricks of the thorn sunk deep into His flesh playing a painful tune all around the crown of His head, like the mournful sound of a piano. Some of the tips of the thorns had broken off on His skull as they pressed it down and these controlled the foot pedal of this piano. Painful! Very painful! The blood and sweat drained into His half-blinded eyes but He could not wipe it; His hands were nailed, literally. They had their own act in this orchestra of pain and agony.

The cruelty of all these men was astonishing, beyond expression. They saw how flayed His back was; how weak He was from the loss of blood, yet they gave Him His cross to carry and mocked Him as He fell under the weight. They realized He had no energy to take another step as He lay there totally exhausted with the cross on top of Him. He had no power to lift it off if He used all His remaining human energy, yet after this they still placed the crown of thorns on His head. Cruel, ferocious, angry, punishing; it was difficult to contemplate the reality He was about to face as He prayed there at Gethsemane.

Just the thought of blood spewing from the holes that the thorns would make is enough to break others. Then a thought came to Him. A thought that was ten times more painful than the reality of the punishment of His body. "I will be wounded in the house of My friends!" That was so hard to digest, so heart-wrenching that He placed His focus on the crucifixion. It was less painful. He knew that He would be wounded time and again by those He loved, those He died to save, those He sacrificed Himself for. It pained Him so much. It was easier to focus on His lifting up, but it would not be easy.

He saw it; it was difficult. He grimaced as He was placed on the cross. The unflinching soldiers came with large metal nails. One held His hand as another lifted the nail and… "Ahhh! Ahhhhh!" The hammer came down and it was crushing. Not only did He react to the unimaginable suffering of having metal piercing His flesh so cruel and intentional, but the hammer... they hammered His flesh as if it was wood or stone. As the hammer made contact it crushed flesh, veins and nerves and left only a pulp strong enough to hold the nail. His hand was crushed and the pain was so excruciating it needed its own orchestra. His body was borne up by His hands on the nails and every part of His body throbbed…

He could see it prophetically from His place of prayer in the garden. It was unbearable, it was inhumane. The mockery, the assault, the rejection, the pain, the suffering… it was horrendous. He could see His mother through His pain, He committed her to John, His beloved apostle. He smiled as He saw love coming through in spite of the excruciation. His spirit came alive when He switched the focus from Himself in the midst of His own crushing pain. He could see one of the thieves who were crucified with Him mocking Him; the other defended Him and begged for mercy and grace. He smiled as He saw Himself extending the mercy. Once again His love shone above the excruciation His body was experiencing and His spirit came alive. He lived for moments like this. It made the cross bearable. That thief would die the death of a thief but would rise with the righteous as if he never sinned. He could not deny the moment; it was suffering beyond human comprehension: the type of death that nobody wants to die, the type of pain nobody wants to feel. This was torture to its greatest extent, torture that engaged every single nerve in the human body and played them individually to maximum torment. He was dying in pain, shame and heartbreak and the heartless crowd was mocking Him. The torture was physical, emotional and mental.

He smiled again. This time He saw Himself rise above the pain and the difficulty to speak, (He labored to frame a syllable). He saw the love shine from His heart as He embraced and covered them. He looked up to Heaven and said, "Father forgive them; they don't understand." He smiled again. This moment made the pain worth it. In fact, He embraced it.

The cross was nothing. It was a common means of punishment in His day faced boldly by many who were not even brave. No. The cross could not have caused these great drops of blood. He had embraced it long ago. He even had rebuked Peter for trying to divert His destiny. Only one person, Satan, had something to lose by Him suffering as He would and He hated Satan. He would give His body in this battle to permanently punish that wicked devil. He would give His body any time for the human race He so loved; every one of them, even the ones inflicting the pain.

The orchestra of pain that crescendos to a climax in an expression of selfless love is the greatest ending and makes the music not just palatable but rather enjoyable.

That is why so many will sing about the cross and even wear it as an ornament. It would be their memorial of love not pain; or rather, the expression of His love through pain.

Jesus would have done this over and over again if He had to. No, this could not incite the level of agony He felt in prayer. It could not have caused His sweat to become like great drops of blood. But something had.

BACK TO REALITY

Surrendered divinity; took on humanity
Faced the challenges of love
from those who challenged love; the ones
He created
Dishonored, disdained; almost stoned.
Was it the wealth He surrendered?
No! All these were past
Could the great drops of blood then
Be inspired by the cross?

Perhaps the loss of His disciples
They all forsook Him; they fled
The stripes that took flesh or
The thorns in His head?
Betrayal; denial
Rejection, abuse
Pained and heartbroken
Alone and misused

He faced these all at Gethsemane

Conclusion now made
He had spoken about these so freely
With resolve, without pain
Must be something more than physical
A conflict of love
Connecting past to the future
Oh! What could have turned His sweat to
blood!
Could it be...?

The cross would be excruciating, it would be very difficult, very painful and brutal, immensely so. It is a death no one wants to encounter. For most persons, the contemplation would be enough to make the sweat run red. He conquered this in prayer without sweat.

But there was a thought that bothered Him. His face showed obvious pain and His sweat glands became as a sieve. Jesus was sweating. Prayer became an anguishing travail.

After some time, Jesus went to check on His disciples.

If there was ever an hour that Jesus needed support it was in that moment. He had with Him His three generals, three disciples who made up His inner circle. And yet, this was a burden He had to carry alone. They would not understand it but they could connect with His passion and pray. That was His expectation of them that they would pray. But He came after such a passionate outpouring of emotions in prayer and He found them sleeping.

He was alarmed. He could feel the darkness closing in and He was concerned about them. If only believers knew the storms threatening them in the spirit, they would saturate the night hours with prayer until their souls are satiated and steal time from the day to pray also. He knew what they did not know. These coming days would be Hell's assault on their Master but would be havoc and misery for them also. Their lives, their livelihood, their future, their faith, their very existence would be shaken and severely threatened. "Men must always pray and never get weary," He sighed. Satan never takes a day off.

He woke them and spoke to Simon and said, "Could you not watch with Me for an hour?" Passion was in His face; His heart was poured out. "If only they could understand!"

He felt compelled to return to His place of prayer. As He prayed, He could see Himself on that cross. Yes, the abuse and the mockery would be leveled at Him. He had no one to turn to; the crowd was hostile.

The mockery, the shame; it was as if they were incited by hell, or perhaps possessed. He could endure this for His abusers. But then, something else bothered Him. A thought which sent shivers through His body every time His mind connected to it.

It was not caused by the physical abuse that he anticipated. These sacrifices were sacrifices of men and He was only spearheading what His followers would endure in time to come. He had already told them the servant is not greater than his master. They would not be exempted. He once told them, "Those who seek to save their life will lose it, but those who are willing to give up their lives for My sake and for the gospel will save it."

No this was not about the physical torment; there were people after Him who immediately after His death would go through similar persecution. They would be killed, thrown in prison, burned, stoned, beaten, thrown off cliffs; given to wild beasts… No, facing death would not bring tears to His eyes or sweat to His brow. But…

He left His three generals praying and returned to His place of prayer some distance away. There was a thought that He could not shake. It made His sweat glands open and created a spring that pumped salted water to His forehead. This thought had Him.

He prayed, and He prayed, and His sweat poured. It was a passionate moment because He could see Himself on the cross, but He could not see Himself anymore. In fact, what He saw was someone He could no longer connect with. What He saw was someone He could not identify. What He saw, was not even a person. What He saw was…

He would go through this all alone. Three years of mentoring would mean nothing in this moment. But then a thought consoled Him. "I can endure because My Father is with Me. He will never leave Me." .

He felt such solace as He thought about His Father and literally felt His presence and comfort in the moment.

It was not long before He had told His disciples that they would all be scattered, each taking His own path to preserve himself. He did tell them He'd be left alone. Then He comforted Himself and said, "I won't be alone. My Father is with Me."

His thoughts in that moment were Good. He had taught them saying, "I and My Father are One." When others fail as long as I have My God beside Me I am alright.

Yet a thought persisted and disturbed Him greatly.

It was not about His relationship with God for His relationship with God was great; very great in the present and He would do nothing to change that.

He remembered saying to Thomas, "If you see Me you see My Father for I and My Father are One." This was a human death and everything was good as long as

His Father was with Him. The connection remained strong between them; rather inseparable.

But then, this thought troubled Him and refused to go away so He prayed, and prayed, and the sweat popped up on His brow. It was humid. His prayer was more than just a prayer but a deep travail that touched every core of His being.

What could it be that changed the color of the sweat to red? What could it be that caused Him to agonize so much that His blood poured from His sweat glands in a mixture that dropped to the earth like crimson rain?

Again He saw Himself on the cross and what He saw was someone He could not identify. What He saw, was not even a person. What He saw was… yes he saw the devil; He saw Satan. The tremors went through His body, because He knew that what He saw in the person of the devil was Himself.

BOOK 3

THE SWEAT AND THE BLOOD

JESUS IS SIN: REPULSIVE

Even the sinful detested Him
Though they could not understand why
They spat at Him and mocked Him
They hated Him by sight
They were incited to do damage
For He was indicted for love and condemned but
they wanted Him to suffer as never before
Though the reason they hated Him so
None could really tell for sure

There was an evil garment placed on Him
In the spirit that none could see
It made them angry with Him
Like a furious nest of bee
They knew that He was innocent
But He did not have a plea

There is a garment which men wear
In it they can do nothing to win
It is weighty and restrictive
It is the garment stained with sin

But the conflict of sin is in becoming the unbecoming
And the load was placed on Him

The thought of the title of this chapter to many is loathsome, detestable, abominable, repulsive, abhorrent, nauseating, disgusting, revolting, vile. There is no reasonable basis of associating the two, Jesus and sin. There is no comparison, no simile, no reconciliation…

But there was a thought that bothered Him. His face showed obvious pain and His sweat glands became as a sieve.

~~~~~~~

"Help, help!" The sound was coming from an open area adjacent to the yard. Jason went to take a look and was surprised to see what appeared to be a change in the landscape. Something was sticking up in the air and there was an opening that he never knew existed.
~~~~~~~

"Help, help!" The voice sounded as if it was choking; choking on something.

Jason quickly ran in the direction of the open pit where the sound was coming from and the smell literally knocked him off his feet. The pungent stench of whatever it was, filled his nostrils and saturated his taste builds immediately. It checked him like a projectile landing on a brick wall.

"Help, help!" The desperation in the voice as it gagged caused him to inch closer to the opening. His hand was on his nose, sealing it shut and he hardly dared to breathe. He could see that the concrete slabs covered in debris, that he walked on frequently, had given way. It had in fact covered a cesspool. The cesspool was open and someone was down there.

"That could have been me," he thought and shivered. He ran for help. Help came. They could do nothing. The pit was deep and full of effluent. The person was doing everything to stay afloat and was obviously losing the battle. Someone called the fire service and luckily the man was still alive when they came. They could hear him struggling. His struggle must have been the most miserable one as every movement forced feces into his system. The fire service was not prepared for this. The effluent was too much. The smell too repulsive (that word again). They called a sewage company. The struggles and the noise had stopped by the time the trucks arrived. It was obvious that the man had died in feces. Had drowned in it. What a way to die! They were able to retrieve the body after the cesspool company had sufficiently drained the effluent from the pit.

Jason shivered as he remembered the sight of the body they recovered. He was covered from head to toe. Feces was in his mouth, his nostrils, his ears, his eyes, his pockets, his hair and all over his body. So repulsive was the sight that no one wanted to touch it even after they had sufficiently washed it off with a hose and poured disinfectant on it. They recognized it was the body of the beloved gardener who had been very unlucky. One pastor who was called was overheard saying, "Makes my skin crawl. Feels just like sin."

Someone commented, "Who could be covered in sin in this way!"

The conversation and drama may be a stretch of the imagination but the story is a true story that took place in a community of the beloved Caribbean jewel, Jamaica.

Yes, as He prayed in the Garden of Gethsemane, there was a thought that bothered Him…

~~~~~~~

Her screams could be heard a mile away. Her captors laughed to themselves as they drove away. "Soften her up a bit so she signs over everything." They would come for her tomorrow. She was in a remote forest and would have no help tonight. She could see the slithering of the black reptiles all around her. They covered the floor of the pit she was in. They were crawling over each other and on the walls. They were so many, she could not move without stepping on them. They crawled up her legs and she screamed. They were non-venomous but it made no difference.
~~~~~~~

They made her skin crawl. (That term again.) She would definitely not sleep that night. She would not dare to lie down or to close her eyes. The thought of them crawling all over her started a strange reaction in her body. She screamed! The temperature was hot but her sweat glands were never told; they opened up and poured cold water. she kept screaming. This was a living misery. It was hell.

After some time of living in her hell ordeal, perhaps two hours, she felt something on her face. Her screams reached a crescendo that was considered to be beyond human capacity. To the normal ear it sounded sinister. She maintained it for a few minutes. It was only after her voice gave way and she paused that she heard it. It was a human voice. It gently but urgently said, "Place the rope over your head and under your armpit."

It was a rope. The past hours had made her feel that anything the snakes desired was possible. When she felt the rope at first she thought that somehow snakes were raining from the sky at her. The panic attack would continue throughout her rescue. She managed to obey the instructions after some trials. She was so nervous. The brain had ceased to function and it was the most difficult instructions to obey. As her feet were lifted from the bottom of the pit there were snakes coiled on her legs. She could not believe she was being rescued. It was as if she was in a dream, hallucinating. She passed out as she was pulled up.

As she came back to her senses, she could feel something touching her feet. She screamed and came awake to the warm hospital bed. A nurse was inspecting the bruises. Her eyes adjusted to the uniform of police officers. The ordeal was over but would never be forgotten. The pit of snakes was the most abominable, detestable, evil and frightful thing one could encounter. Well at least for her.

It gives one a hormonal reaction like the general reaction to the title of this chapter: Jesus is Sin.

The author thought of the woman who slept in the same bed as her rotting mother every day for three weeks after she died. He vomited. He thought of the woman in the Bible who ate her son because of the famine and retched again.

He thought of humans going to hell and having to live with all those demons in that place. One demon is enough to make your environment vile. Their very nature is revolting. Look what they do to anyone they possess. To live with them is worse than falling in a pit full of snakes or drowning in a cesspool.

His thoughts took him back to Jesus in the Garden of Gethsemane. There was a thought that bothered Jesus. It was not the fear of death, rejection or even losing His disciples. So what was it? His face showed obvious pain and His sweat glands became as a sieve. Could it be that it was not the feeling of fear but rather the dread of something repulsive that triggered this reaction? Could it be as torturous as the thought of drowning in a cesspool, covered in effluent, like a sinner covered in sin? Well…is there something to that simile?

THE THOUGHT THAT MADE HIM SWEAT

BECOMING THE UNBECOMING

Nothing to do with it
Not even a thought
No association, no conversation
No liking, not one inkling or an aught
Nothing in it for Me
Nothing in Me for it
Not neutral about it
To hate it passionately
Yet to be forced to marry it
To put it on and to carry it
To forsake yourself and to become it
What greater mental anguish could there ever
be?

Jesus did everything to rise above the shame, the pain and the punishment of the cross, but one thought repeatedly crushed Him. He resigned Himself to the cross and was even slain before the earth was created but He could not resign Himself to this. The crucifixion had taken place in heaven long time ago or rather before time, but, not what He was about to face. He had to face it and conquer it in the Garden of Gethsemane. It was something He knew was coming, not something He could ever come to terms with. He prayed, "Father, if there is ever a possibility for You to do it another way, take this cup away from Me."

It was something He had no strength or courage to face. It was something he had no power to flee. It was something that made any pretense of courage berserk. If is something you flee from if you can and you pray would flee from you if you cannot. It is a cup that only God could compel you to drink and even then you plead with Him to take it away.

His voice was lifted up as His sweat poured, "Father, if it is possible…if it can happen otherwise…"
Why did Jesus see in that moment of prayer that inspired such a reaction?

Ahhhhh!
Nothing to do with it
Not even a thought
No association, no conversation
No liking, not one inkling or an aught
Nothing in it for Me
Nothing in Me for it
Not neutral about it
To hate it passionately
Yet to be forced to marry it
To put it on and to carry it
To forsake yourself and to become it
What greater mental anguish could there ever
be?

It was sin, no longer enticing Him but grabbing Him and forcing Him to wear its evil, slithery, filthy, detestable, abominable, repulsive self like a skin-hugging cloak. He would have no power to resist it. He was about to take the sins of the entire world on Himself. Isaiah 53:12 says, "He bore the sins of many." Verse 8 says He was stricken for the transgressions of My people. The contrast in verse 9 is that He was never violent and there was no deceit in His mouth. He never sinned. I Cor 15:3 asserts He died for our sins. Galatians 1:4 states that He gave Himself for our sins. I John 2:2 states that He satisfied the demands of our sins. IJohn 3:5 says He came to take our sins away. Revelation 1:5 says He washed our sins in His own blood.

Indeed, the moment had caught up with Him and it was heavy. For Him to fulfill this role as propitiation for sins, or to wash our sins, He first had to bear our sins. He could not do it from a distance, otherwise He would have done it from heaven. He had to wear it.

He had nothing to do with sin. He never sinned. He hated sin and everything that had to do with the devil. The thought of dishonoring His Father or offending love was repulsive. It was worse for Him than any of the propositions we examined above. He could bear human punishment but not this. He was the beloved Son of the Father who pleased His Father well. The thought of displeasing Him made Him want to retch.

No, the sin He bore was not His, I Peter 2:24 states it was ours. Hebrews 1:3 states it was ours. This was a spiritual transaction that all human punishment combined required. Hebrews 4:15 states that He was tempted in every way we are yet He never sinned. The thought of bearing all the sins He so hated mesmerized Him in His place of prayer in the garden. He could not control Himself at this thought. All His senses reacted. His nerve repelled. His stomach turned, and He sweated as if under severe torture, and He was. He was to take on all the murders, the witchcraft, the child abuse, the perversion, the prostitution, the drug addiction, the genocide, the cannibalism, the satanic ritual abuse, the wickedness, the lies, stealing, hatred, unforgiveness, fear, backbiting, idolatry, betrayal; all of the sins of all the world to include yours.

And if this was bad, it was about to get worse. This probably would have made Him sweat a little. Bearing sin on His righteous soul. But that was not it. No. There is a bitter twist to the story. I Peter 2:24

captures it very well. It states, "He Himself bore our sin in His own body."

No, the sin that He bore was not His nor was it a garment He wore; it was placed in His own body not on it. It was a garment that wore Him. It took away His personality and gave Him its own. The severity of the matter was such that He was not only to take on sin but He was to become it.

Paul was more blatant about it in 2 Corinthians 5:21, he stated that God made Jesus who knew no sin to become sin for us. Again in Galatians 3:13, he also asserts that Christ has redeemed us from the curse, becoming Himself a curse for us, for according to the scriptures everyone who hangs on a tree is cursed. They have not only borne curses but they have become a curse.

The thought of becoming sin was overbearing. His body repelled. He recognized that there was no escape. This was the punishment of all punishment. Torture above torture. He prayed a simple prayer, "Father, if only it is possible..."

Yes, it was prophesied that the iniquities of all, every person would be laid on Him. The iniquity of the entire world. Every sin and transgression against His Father that had ever been committed and would ever be committed. No, He would not just take all of this weight of sin, He would become it. He would be the transgressor against His loving Father and the object of His hatred. He knew His own passionate hatred for sin. He remembered His reaction in the temple as the religious leaders allowed it to be defiled. These were the same emotions He was battling with, only now He was the object of the anger. He could not describe it; He was becoming angry with Himself because of the sin. Feelings could not describe what He was going through. It was such a conflict as He had to become the offense and the offender. The thought of this was excruciating. It was the greatest pain that anyone could feel because it had no solution. It was torment beyond torment. It was so surreal and so unreal. This was unbearable. It was intolerable. He was mind-boggling. It was a punishment He was not ready for. As He processed this in prayer, He felt the pain in His heart. Was it not written that cursed is everyone who hung on a tree? He would become the curse… Jesus, a curse. He knew it. He knew what it meant to become a curse. There is no curse that has a place in the presence of God, partnership with God, communion with God, He knew it; it caused such strange reactions in His body that He just could not explain or come to grips with it.

In that moment, He would take on the personality of the devil. This was the greatest pain. "Ahhh, the devil! Me! I have nothing to do with the devil; nothing to do with Satan and his sustained rebellion." The devil was as far away and as distant from Him as light was from darkness, as good from evil; as oil from water. Just the very thought of the devil and his rebellion brought repulsion (that word again) to Him. The thought that He would take on all this corruption was sickening and frightening; it was frighteningly sick. It was worse than the thought of being put in a pit filled with crawling snakes. Whether they were poisonous or not, it doesn't matter. Just the thought of being there makes your skin crawl. It was worse than the fate of the man in the cesspool, drowned in human waste, ingesting it, covered in it; drowning in it. He was to become the filth. He would have changed from the fragrance of heaven to the filth of the earth. This was even more stifling than the evil fate of that man who died in the cesspool filled with filth. No, nothing could compare to what it felt to take on the devil's personality. Nothing could prepare Him for this. You cannot become the devil's personality without standing against God. Jesus agonized there and the sweat poured. This was a fight that did not belong to Him, yet He knew spiritual things confuses human understanding and this was the only way to win the battle of sin in the spiritual. Sin needed a propitiation, it needed a resolve and it would accept no other terms.

The thought of any person living forever with hateful and wicked Satan and all his demons in one place should make any human shudder. One person living with a demon is a complete wreck: madness, nastiness, poverty, pain, confusion, aggression. Life is always downhill fast once the devil is involved. The thought of becoming the devil was inconceivable yet this was His reality. There was no way to beat the devil at His game of sin than to become who He was and what He does, sin. But this meant He had to resign Himself to the thought of hurting Someone He loved above all things. The thought of representing all the hurts that have been targeted to Him in the past and present; the hurts He too had received being one with Him.

"Father if it is possible…" It was painful, so painful. It was unbearable, excruciating. The thought of taking the personality of the devil was something more than He could imagine.

"If it was possible," He pleaded with the Father. "Father, if it is possible, take this cup from Me."

For He had:

Nothing to do with
Not even a thought
No association, no conversation
No liking, not one inkling or an aught
Nothing in it for Me

Nothing in Me for it
Not neutral about it
To hate it passionately
Yet to be forced to marry it
To put it on and to carry it
To forsake yourself and to become it
What greater mental anguish could there
ever be?

*No!! He had nothing to do with it but it had everything
to do with Him and there was nothing He could do
about it.*

It was not His own sin that He was taking on, it was the sins of the entire world: the sin of every murderer, adulterer, prostitute or drug dealer, the sin of those who have committed mutilations, every child abuser, liar, deceiver, fraudulent person. The sin of every witch, wizard, warlock, cannibal, every wicked person and every abominable and hateful person on the face of the earth would fall upon Him and He would take their personality on the cross. He would become them. This was unbearable.

This was, oh… "Father if it is possible…"

This caused His sweat glands to become springs and the sweat to pour in great drops, but even then it did not cause His blood vessel to burst. There was something else. There was something in His past that was there in His present that He had to face in His future. Something indescribable. Something He had to cling to which was being forced away from Him by His own acceptance and free will gift… well, if that is reconcilable. Then again, perhaps this moment of trepidation was irreconcilable. What could be worse for this righteous Man than becoming sin?

They were not of equal significance
But the trigger; the cause
One triggered the other
He could not escape at all
The one He took on; (the one He became)
Would cause in the end
The other to put Him off; (because of what had
become Him)
And release Him as equal and a friend
He had no retreat, no answer
No words to describe
Where His voice failed for speech
Blood fell into His eyes

As Jesus prayed, He came to a place of settlement, a place of resignation where He had peace. His Spirit was never settled but even in the midst of His agony He resigned Himself to God's will. It was then He heard a cry that startled and unsettled Him. The words were barely legible because it was filled with such pain. The words had more of an effect than anything. It echoed through every part of His body and reverberated in His bones like a painful echo that refused to abate. It was filled with so much misery that the only word He could hear was, "Why…?"

The voice that cried was His voice. The words caused so much pain inside that it was tangible and piercing. It felt like a dagger to His heart, frozen in eternity. It was the type of pain that made you seek the death exit but the tenacious pain that refused to permit the quick escape of death. He looked on the ground and saw a red spot on a leaf below His face. It was watery blood. The realization came that it was coming from His face. Even then the agony was too great, weaponizing each thought with what felt like an electric shock. He wasn't even allowed to wrap His thoughts around it.

He found solace in the midst of the pain by diverting from the pain and thinking about His Father. His heart took Him back to His own words. He was speaking to the crowd and the agitated Pharisees telling them, "I and My Father are one."

He made this assertion again in the presence of His disciples, "If you knew Me you would have known the Father also; from now on you know Him; you have seen Him."

Phillip was not satisfied, he said, "Show us the Father and we will be satisfied."

Jesus could hear Himself responding, "I have spent so much time with you yet you don't know Me, Phillip. Everyone who have seen Me have seen the Father. Why are you asking Me to show you the Father then? Is it that you do not believe that I am in the Father and He in Me. I don't speak of My own disposition or authority; the Father in Me does all the works I do. If only for the works sake, believe that I am in the Father and He in Me."

Another time He said, "I of Myself do nothing, I only do what My Father teaches Me."

Jesus and His Father were not synchronized or coordinated, they are one Person with separate personalities. All the earth had come to accept this. They pray to the Father and to Jesus interchangeably. Some, wanting to be precise prays to the Father in the name of Jesus. Jesus Himself once said, "If anyone prays to the Father in His name, I will answer."

By revelation the Apostle John would state, there are three who bear witness in heaven, the Father, the Word and the Spirit and these three are one. He had already clarified in the first chapter of John that the Word is the Son. Jesus took solace in the midst of His pain by reaching into the comforting presence of His Father. No, He was not alone. He once told His disciples predicting the coming moments, "You will all be gone; You will leave Me alone, but I am not alone, My Father is with Me."

These were comforting thoughts. It consoled Him as He prayed and agonized.

Then He heard it again. It was a cry of greatest horror. It was more like a shriek that penetrated His blood vessels and made them burst into His sweat glands. He recognized the voice; it was His. This is what caused blood to pump into His sweat. This moment was so unnatural, it compelled an unnatural response from His

body. This time the words were very distinct, "My God, My God, why…why have You forsaken Me."
He was inconsolable. The torture was horrendous and He had no answer.

How could that be possible? It was inconceivable, unthinkable and equally unbearable. This time the color of the sweat changed completely. There was so much inner activity, the sweat that was pouring from Him was like great drops of blood.

What transpired in that moment is often glossed over, but was the real spiritual sacrifice of the cross. We are about to examine it.

To live the life of the crucified
Though but a child He be
This is My beloved Son
In His I am well pleased
He did everything that one could do
To please the Father's heart
He was perfect in obedience
In Him there was no fault

What then could have caused
The Father to push Him off
And in His time of greatest need
To turn His back and block His heart?

When Jesus took the sins of the world upon Himself; His greatest fear was realized. He could endure anything but He took comfort in the connection with the Father. He was so intimately connected with God that any break in that relationship would devastate Him. But to please this God,

He had to bear the sins of man. God can have nothing to do with sin. He literally had to turn His back on Jesus when He became sin. This was the thing Jesus saw in the Garden that caused the reaction in His body. This was the essence of His very being that was about to disintegrate. This was His past, in His present that would not be present in His future, at least in that moment. For Jesus, this was all the blows the cross had to offer. Nothing could have pained Him worse. It would be the only time heaven would block its ear to Him.

There is a victory that can never win
When victory is marred with sin
When they matter most
You matter not
When your earth is blood and your heavens
blocked

The implications of this are far reaching and breaches all principles itself. God is righteous and can have nothing to do with sin, even if it is on His own self, His Son.

> Love sent you; love led you
> Love brought you to the spot
> The Love you fought for withdrew from you
> When the battle raged extremely hot

The poets wrote about this moment in many different ways:

> The Love you needed
> Withdrew, retreated
> Although you pleaded
> He turned His back

Another poet argued that Jesus was the last person God would turn His back on. He did nothing but love God. Everything He went through was to please God. The poet wrote:

You suffered for love
Your blood spattered for love
With shame covered for love
Yet for love you poured out your care
Spat on for love
Despised, bruised and battered for love
Held up both hands for love
When your heart beckoned for love
Love was not there
Love left you in despair

God is righteous and walking away from love and faithfulness as that of His Son's must have pained Him greatly. He had no option. He could have nothing to do with sin.

The poet wrote:

There is a victory that can never win
Victory that is marred by Sin
Though your victory makes others brag
And give them what they never had
It leaves you out of your own show

Facing God's wrath and in the cold
Bruised, battered, broken, hurt and… alone
Bruised and alone
Battered and alone
Broken and alone
Hurting and all alone
Oh, so very much alone…

God, turning His back on Jesus who did nothing but obey, please and honor Him, because of the sin He carried is a lesson for the self-righteous. This debunks the argument that many give that they do not have to follow the way of Christ, confess Him, connect with believers, but God understands because they do good. They serve God in their own way. Good is not an excuse for God. There was none as good as Jesus. If God turned away from Jesus because He had sin on Him, our sins, why should He accept you with your own sin? Should He then accept you with all your good if you ignore the sacrifice His Son made for you?

This also leads to a greater and more earth-shattering revelation. It means that the suffering could not be on the cross alone; the Father must have suffered tremendously also. Could it be that the greater part of the sacrifice did not take place on the cross? Is it possible that the Bible was deliberate when it described the sacrifice in John 3:16 without mentioning the cross?

Could this meant that God had to split Himself in two and allow half of Him to die on the cross so that all of Him could be reconciled to man. If Jesus and the Father is one, then how do you divide one and when you divide one but any whole but one, what do you get? A fraction. Could it be that God was a fraction of Himself when Jesus became sin?

BOOK 4

THE UNSEEN SACRIFICE

THE REAL SACRIFICE OF THE CROSS

LOVE

If you want to learn the real depth
of this extravagant sacrificial gift
Try taking the heart out of your body
and then expect to live
Cut your feet off
and try to take a step
Take the lungs out of your body
and try taking a breath
Take the sun out of the day
And expect things to be the same
Take the children from a mother
And tell her not to pain
Take the Son out of the Father
And place Him on the cross
And expect heaven to be normal
And the Father nonchalant and relaxed

The oneness of the Godhead was to be tested on the cross, rather, it was to be sacrificed on the cross. This was the only time God hid Himself from Jesus. Their relationship was too strong; too perfect. The only thing that could break this relationship was God's love for mankind as dictated in John 3:16. This was the agony, the real sacrificial, blood-dripping agony of the cross. When Jesus took on the sin of all mankind, God would literally turn His back on Jesus, the Father on the Son, love on love, so He could turn His face to you. God literally ripped His heart out in order to make you this love offering. And He did it. That was the real sacrifice of the cross and it took place in heaven not on earth. Love had to split Himself in two and despise one half in order to offer what sin demanded.

The Garden of Gethsemane was His part
The blood spilt from His raptured heart
But the Father's heart bled on the cross
Where love should help but love could not
Where love easy was made hard to love
Where true love meant discarded love
And love faithful not rewarded love

Where the love for man retarded love
And love deliberately ruptured love
So love could pour this love on us

It is impossible to imagine what took place in heaven while Jesus took our sins on the cross. For God to turn His back on His Son, His only begotten Son, the one whom He loved; in whom He was well pleased, it must have been the greatest tragedy of heaven.

It is easy to look at the physical without seeing the spiritual reality of what had actually taken place before our eyes. Jesus died on the cross but it was the Father who gave Him. He did this because He so loved the world. This is why Jesus deferred the final decision to Him, saying, "Not My will but Yours."

The giving of the Son was as great a sacrifice as the resignation of the Son to the will of the Father. It is hard to imagine how the angels beholding the face of God must have reacted watching Him complete the sacrifice in heaven. The only time in history Love had to betray itself; to split in two to make a moment happen; the moment of salvation.

Nothing split in two remains the same. Split a nation in two it gets weaker. Split a family in two it loses strength. Split an engine in two it ceases to work. Power split in two loses impact. That is why there are so many benefits from cooperation, collaboration and teamwork at all levels. Nations cooperate for greater impact. NATO, EU, WTO, UN are some examples. Love split in two is like a heart split in two. The pain was unbearable but the impact was about to be tested at the highest level.

Jesus was slain from the foundation of the world but there was something that did not take place until the cross; it was His separation from God; love from love. Jesus anticipated this in the garden with travailing pain.

The story of a cross is the story of Love turning its back on Love to embrace love. It is the story of God literally splitting Himself in two, and literally detesting half of Himself so that He could embrace all of us. It is a story where Christ did not have a cry on the cross, did not have a call, where the heavens were shut up to Him, where He was shut out like a filthy rag. Where the Father could not bear the sight of Him because sin was not only on Him, He had become sin. That is the true story of the cross; it was not just a painful death.

The thought of Love splitting in two is surreal. Love that is perfect, love that is pure, had to turn on love, in the name of love for the cause of love of this entire world. When we understand that sacrifice that took place on the cross, we appreciate that this pain was greater in heaven than it was on Earth. The pain of love. God Himself went through the punishment, for God is love. Never before has it been recorded that agape turns its back on someone who in all perfection lived to honor love. It is all-round and complete torture for Love to turn His back on Love when Love did nothing wrong, nothing but to love Him with tenacious emphatic obedience and perform His will to complete perfection. This was the unbearable, unthinkable, unimaginable, unmanageable agonizing pain of the garden. His human will would have turned away. This was more than human suffering and above human sacrifice. It was the time the love for His Father took precedence. He said, "Not My will but Yours."

This made the pain of the Father even more excruciating. The only fault anyone could find in Him was complete obedience and love for the Father. This was heaven's pain. It was heaven's sacrifice, hardly ever spoken about. Parents understand how it feels to turn your back on children in trouble, good or bad. None can turn their back on a child that is completely obedient and extravagant in loving them. There is none who knows how to return love like God and to love even when He is not loved. The prophet Hosea is His example; this moment in time was another. God had to turn His back on His good Son, the Son He loved in His greatest pain on the cross because His will was that Jesus remained there to bear the sins of men to set them free.

For God so loved the world that He gave is very weighty. God loved the world so much, it had to take a special love, an unbelievable supernatural love for Him to do this to Someone who is totally innocent and fully in love with Him. A love that burned away from His Son and towards humanity. A sacrifice that needed the selfless surrender of a willing and obedient Son in order to fulfill.

It was somewhat like the submission of Isaac so Abraham could express his love and fear for God.

For Jesus this was painful. It was a time the earth hated Him and His heavens were brass. Everyone targeted Him with offenses. They all did Him evil. They accused Him, denied Him in His innocence, condemned Him in His innocence, afflicted Him in His innocence, mocked and abused Him in His innocence, now God... now God Himself whom He loved with every bit of strength, every thought of His heart, every organ inside Him and every passion in His soul; whose presence He relied on in His darkest hour; whose relationship He felt secure in; whose energy and heart He was channeling; who was one with Him… now God turned His back on Him. This is the true sacrifice of the cross. It is about what took place at Calvary, but greater yet, what took place in heaven.

If love is love, then love can have no ordinary reaction to its own pain.

For love to turn away love, is a contradiction

When all love did was follow His directions

To see the bitterness of everyone toward Him
And to know He was their sin offering
But to turn Himself away it pained
And to block His ear when He heard His name,
"My Father…"
Wanting to help but He was restrained
Love is never easy, but this one really drained.

In heaven, the powerful angels stood by powerless, unable to help. Angels who worshiped and revered Jesus stood by and watched. They could not intervene. If Jesus had called, the Father would have permitted and they would have responded because they were subject to His call. He had all power with His Father but, love never imposes, it transposes to the heart of the other. Jesus did not call. His Father did not command it. His Father's back was turned on Him. His ears were closed to Him because He was no longer the Son that was united with Him, He was sin and there is no unity of righteousness with sin. It pained heaven. Heaven was in tears if that is permitted. The clouds became dark because there was no purpose for the sun in the heavens to shine in the moment the Son on earth who had given it its glory was crucified. Love itself was brought into confusion and into conflict. It must have been the most impossible and uncomfortable moment in heaven. It pained heaven and could easily have rained the tears of angels for the only time in history that day.

LOVE WINS

The moment the Father turned away from His Son on the cross was unbearable but the objectives were fully achieved. Love had to reach in so that love could reach out. Love given out expands. Love is the glue for effective collaboration and corporation or unity. What the Father knew is that after the punishment of the cross, He would have His Son again with the many who would receive the sacrifice. The more love is given, the more it multiplies. Love is only strong, or rather, love is only love, when it is given away, broken and distributed.

The principle of Love is that it love gets stronger, not weaker, when given out in acts of love. The only way to kill love is to withhold it. Love can never die if given and surrendered to death for love. It only expands. Love is like a seed. It can be planted. Sacrifice for love is never lost; never forgotten. The cross was painful. The separation of Father and Son even more unbearable but it was a sacrifice of Love. God is Love. Love voluntarily split Himself apart in order to multiply this amazing love to everyone.

Love in heaven was restored to perfection, the Father, the Son and the Spirit, after the death of Jesus in His conquest of sin and extended to the many who would be redeemed from sin by this sacrifice.

When there is a crisis of love, perhaps a sacrifice for love is demanded; when love sacrifices it answers any crisis of love.

Love Had to split in two
They could no longer be one
There is no way for God and sin
To be joined hand in hand
Love had to deny, that love was His child
Love had to lose itself so love could multiply
For love is not love unless it is given away
And loves the greatest love
When it extends itself through pain
And love is manifested, when love is truly tested

The Love of the Father is the love the cross
reflected
The cross was a token of the sacrifice in heaven

It pained Love
And shamed love
  Abused, rejected, disdained Love
Pure and innocent yet they blamed Love
Up in heaven above they nailed Love
Everything the Son suffered impaled Love
To turn His back on Love distressed Love
For all the Son went through,
The Father went through it worse
To turn His back on Love crucified,
Hurt love to the core.
But He did it all so He could reclaim love
And that the heavens up above could rain love
The love of His Son on the people of the earth

This is the story of the cross; the real love story was never solely about what transpired on the cross. It was much greater. John 3:16 said nothing about the cross. It is all about what took place in heaven. It is all about love, a real love story which all happened behind the scenes. 'God so loved the world' is a passage with deeper depth and meaning than what is normally spoken and acknowledged. It is not just about the sacrifice by Jesus but the sacrifice by God. It is not just about the gift, but about the pain and heart of the giver. God never spoke to Isaac about his obedience as an offering, He spoke to Abraham and said, "Because you have done this…" The real sacrifice took place in heaven. It was God dissecting Himself, 'Love' to perfect love for all. It is about a God who so loved the world that He gave.

THE CONFLICT OF LOVE

Your Conflict; Your Response

This conflict of love is the conflict of decision everyone faces daily.

It is the conflict that keeps people, believers and unbelievers from surrendering their will to His.

For sinners, we know His will is that you accept Him today in capital letters…TODAY.

Jesus did not wait until it felt good. Honestly, it would never happen. There would never be a moment that it would feel good to carry sin. There would never be a moment that it would feel good to separate from God. He did not wait until the conditions were right. The devil jumps in at hesitation and makes it more complicated. For some unbeliever life is so complicated that only a miracle can make what would have been a simple decision. Some are living in with unmarried spouses, with children, depending on the spouse for support, facing a crisis of love for a person who refuses marriage. Some are in prostitution, possessed, drug addicts, living in life-threatening situations that gets worse if they commit. So many situations.

Jesus did not wait on the situation to change, it hardly ever. He simply surrendered and allowed God to do the rest. He said, "Nevertheless, not my will but Yours…" This is Your sacrifice not mine; just as Isaac did not struggle with tear-filled, soft-hearted Abraham, the only answer is, "I surrender all."

The unbeliever's response

For unbelievers, the question to you is: if God did this for you, if love was willing to split Himself to embrace you; if Jesus went through this just because of you, is it right to continue to hold on to that sin and to keep punishing Love? If Jesus was prepared to go through this just to free you from the bondage that you're in, is it right to tell Him to wait until some other time? Should God punish Himself in the way He suffered as He turned away from Love to embrace you and still wait on you to value His sacrifice and embrace Him in return?

If He was willing to punish Himself to reconcile you with pure Love, is it right to punish Him more and to tell Him, tomorrow? Is it right to hold on to your own ways? If Jesus selflessly gave Himself so that you would not be punished forever how can you say no to Him? Not now?

Not today? How can you say to Him: I am not willing; I am not ready?

This is your moment. Say:
Jesus, I believe that You are the Son of God.
I believe that You came took all my sins on the cross.
I refuse to carry them anymore.
I put the devil to shame and call him defeated in my life.
I accept You as my Lord and Savior.
Be Lord over my situation; I commit it all to You.
May Your grace and mercy speak for me from now on.
Amen.

Find a Bible believing church and submit yourself.
Tell the pastor about your monumental decision to be on the right side of the crisis of the cross.

Next
Read your Bible and pray daily. Have a big appetite and you will overcome big problems easily. A normal reading

is five chapters every day. Be abnormal, read ten or twenty. The cross was not normal.

The Believer's Response

The question to believers is: can it be right to stand by in safety and watch this sacrifice of love go down the drain. Isn't it normal to rise with adrenaline pumping and contend that what God went through will be avenged? How can you sit down and let the devil win in the fight for humanity after what He did to your Lord? Start with your family for instance; list every member you know who is not saved. Irrespective of their condition or addiction, love ripped Himself apart for them. Love them until you are tired and keep loving them. Let them know Jesus is the reason. He will do the rest. In wars against injustice like the Ukraine war many were stirred to volunteer. To put their lives on the line to enter the fray. Are you not stirred to take up arms as soldiers of the cross with one passion, to avenge the cross; energized by the pain Jesus suffered to pour your energy into the heart of the Father, ripped in two for a sinful world? Are you not angry with every stripe Jesus felt; every thorn, every insult, every spit, every rejection? Can't you feel every nail; the broken heart? Will you let the devil get away with it with impunity with the many others He is afflicting with pain, sicknesses and sin today? You see them everywhere; they are Jesus suffering. He said so Himself. They are the cross before you all over again, only that you have the power to enter the game and to crush the devil because of the cross. Loving God with all your strength and mind is to add all your strength, energy and mind into the love that was poured out on the cross. To ensure a day will not pass without your witness. Those who understand the sacrifice and are not moved by love to extend the love is beyond feeling. Every day is another day to be passionate about this Love who went through this much because He was so passionate about us.

The first step in doing so is to commit yourself selflessly to the Lord Jesus Christ, and to say to Jesus, "I commit myself to avenge Your blood. I accept Your sacrifice on the cross. My blood is pumping hot. I am in."

The second step is to spread it; to make a determination that whatever field of life you are in, you will give yourself to the message of the cross. You will not allow God to sacrifice alone. Love split Himself in two, therefore, if you have to split your time in two and to split your priorities you will let Love know that His excruciating sacrifice will not be in vain; that the blood Jesus shed shall not be wasted as long as you are alive. Not one drop of blood spilled will be allowed to be nullified you will gather it with care and extend it to a life. Love split Himself in two to give Himself fully to the redemption of man. Consider what you need to do. God wants to take care of your priorities if you will get a heart for His. You seek the kingdom first and you give Love a chance to reciprocate in the most beautiful and lively relationship with you and others. Love wants to expand and grow; to become an organism in your life through your own sacrifice. It cost God everything to give you Himself; let sacrifice write your love story with Him. Jesus said, Go into all the world." He is needed in your world however it is defined; your family, your community, your village, your business and social circle; your contacts, your interactions, your scope of influence and beyond. Perhaps you were assigned there for such a time as this. Be adamant that you will not wait for opportunities to come to you; you will seek them out.

BOOK 5

WITNESSING WITH THIS REVELATION

In the introduction of this book, I shared about witnessing on Saturdays and the almost perfect response I received to the call for repentance.

This is the story I told.

I will now share with you the short format of the message I shared with those I witnessed to and my approach in two formats. A standard format and a shortened format when you only have a couple of minutes.

MY PRESENTATION STANDARD

Step I: Use a good introduction.

I simply asked: *May I pray for you?*

This introduction is good for Jamaica with a very religious population. They will hardly resist a prayer. I have found that it does not matter how hardened the person is, they will stop everything for prayer. In fact, the more hardened the person is, the more they desire prayer and are appreciative of the outreach. I have witnessed to prostitutes, rough-looking men (one was in tears as I prayed and told me he went to an obeah man the day before), and everyone else just by simply asking offering prayer. I once stopped a police sergeant in the midst of a road check and held his hand and prayed.

Step 2: *Ask their name and Pray for them*

Some may be reluctant to give their name at first but pray.

Release grace to their business, career, speak life to their bodies; health to their relationships and family; break demonic assignments against their life and generational curses. Speak a turnaround.

This is an example:

By the power in the blood of Jesus, I release angels to you right now. I speak that you shall prosper. You shall succeed in everything You do. I break generational curses and every evil assignment against your life. I speak by the power of the living God that you shall prosper; your relationships shall flourish. The hand of the enemy against your family is broken. I speak health to your body. I commit you to the Lord. Your name is recorded in heaven for angelic assignment.

This will create an opening for a short word.

Step 3: Give the short message: <u>Great Drops of Blood.</u>
Make it conversational.

This is the full message which takes between 5 and 7
minutes.

THE MESSAGE: GREAT DROPS OF BLOOD

The Bible in Luke 22:44 said that Jesus was in so much agony that His sweat became as great drops of Blood.

Can you imagine someone in so much pain that His blood vessels burst in the sweat glands and poured on the earth?

Jesus was about to be betrayed and to be crucified and He was in deep agony. For His sweat to become blood, something must have bothered Him to the extent that His organs and vessels rebelled.

What do you believe caused Jesus to agonize so much?

Give a few seconds for an answer.

Could it be the extreme sacrifice of leaving heaven? To put off His divinity and becoming flesh?

This is very significant because in the flesh He could be tempted. What do you believe would have happened if He had sinned? He would never have returned. He placed His divinity on the line to embrace humanity.

To come to earth meant He would also be maltreated. He would suffer abuse at the hand of the men He created. They called Him Beelzebub, they tried to stone Him; to push Him off a cliff. Could this be what bothered Him so much in the garden?

Well no! at the time He was in the garden, He had already come to earth and suffered all these things. It was not what was past but something still to come.

What then could have caused the great drops of blood?

Most will say the suffering of the cross.

Use the opportunity to amplify the pain of the cross.

Could it be the physical suffering of His crucifixion? Well, could it be? Indeed, the cross would be excruciating. The entire process was unimaginable pain and heartache.

First the rejection.

Everyone would reject Him. the same people He ministered to, who followed Him all the time; who were healed; who cried Hosanna when he made His entry to Jerusalem would hurl abuse at Him and join the crowd saying, "Crucify Him." His disciples would not be there in His moment of greatest pain. They would betray Him, deny Him and desert Him. That can hurt.

Have you ever been rejected? How about rejection by someone close to you? Lied on, betrayed, forsaken? That is intense emotional hurt.

He had to be rejected so He could associate with yours.

The heart of Jesus was completely broken in the end but the cross was not just emotional and mental torture, it was extreme physical torture and abuse.

First He was whipped. Can you imagine someone whipped so much that their back was physically ripped, blood spewing from it? The Cato-nine whip has the reputation of having bits of metal in the end to ensure every contact punctured the flesh. The scars would never leave the back. Then He was compelled to carry His cross. He was so physically depleted after the whipping that He fell under the weight of the cross. It Had no strength to move another step. It was beyond the physical capacity of His human body. And it was not over:

They placed a crown of thorns on His head, pressed down to make His head fiery painful? Have you ever had a thorn break in your flesh? Can you imagine multiple thorns at the same time; and on your head, many breaking on your skull?

Then He was hung up by His hands. If a hammer touches your hand it is extremely painful. Can you imagine it coming at intentional speed and power driving a nail? The flesh must have been crushed as the nail joined it to the wood. Then to be left there on the weight of the nails until you expire. The entire body must have ached to the very end.

The knowledge of this would be enough to make anyone sleepless and sweat all night. Jesus knew what was to take place in advance and He spoke about it often to His disciples.

Then there would be abuse. He not only died innocently, wrongfully, but He was mocked, spit on, buffeted and slapped. Have you ever been in such a situation where you were accused and punished wrongly?

Don't you believe that would be more than enough to make His sweat blood?

Most people would agree.

That death on the cross was common in His day. It was the normal punishment for ordinary thieves. Also the followers of Jesus were to go through extreme torture for Him. They would do so bravely, even joyfully. He was no coward. There was something more. What could it be?

At this you will have piqued their interest.

Continue your story:

When Jesus was nailed to the cross He took the sins of the world to Himself. Can you imagine all the sins you yourself have committed, lies, hatred, forgiveness, betrayal, immorality; plus the sin of everyone else, murders, drug pushers, child abusers, prostitutes, perversion, genocide, witches, idolaters everything? The Bible says in 2 Corinthians 5:21 that He did not just take the sin of everyone but God made Him sin for us.

Jesus had never sinned. He has nothing to do with the devil. The very thought of sin was disgusting to Him. It must have been the most repulsive thing He could imagine. It is like taking a bath in a cesspool. Like falling in a pit of crawling snakes. Like the most nauseating thing you can imagine. The thought of becoming the thing He hated most must cause His stomach to turn and His face to sweat in mental anguish.

But that was not all. It still does not explain the blood in His sweat. So what caused the blood?

When Jesus took the sins of the world to Himself God would turn His back on Him, literally. He knew this. He hated sin and God hated sin. If He became sin He would be object of the hatred of God. God has nothing to do with sin. He would turn His back on Him literally. His own Son, innocent and obedient. He must have heard the cry, "My God, My God why have You forsaken Me?" His own voice vocalizing the unfathomable.

Jesus had prophesied to His disciples that they would all forsake Him but He was not alone for God was with Him. He had also said openly to the disgust of the Jews, "I and My Father are one". Can you imagine what it feels to have the earth turn on you and have heaven closed to you at the same time?

For Jesus it was much more than this; He was one with God. He was about to lose His identity altogether, His association, His refuge; His call. He was to become something He absolutely hated and something that had no voice before the one He absolutely loved.

That is more than enough to make sweat turn to blood.

Now there is no one as good as Jesus. If God turned His back on Jesus on the cross because He had sin on Him, will He accept those who do good but reject the sacrifice of Jesus on the cross? Certainly not!

That made His sweat blood but it is not the end of the story. The greater sacrifice took place in heaven. The sacrifice of God; the sacrifice of love.

Can you imagine what it must have felt for God to see His Son suffer so much and do nothing? Can you imagine what it took for God to turn His back on Jesus who became sin just to do His will? If you have children you will understand that you will not see them in pain and not get involved, even if they are guilty. Moreover, if the child has done nothing but love you and do whatever you desire of them. Would it not break you up completely to turn away from that child in their greatest need and pain?

How much more for God whose love is perfect and who did not just love His Son but was one with Him?

This sacrifice tore heaven in two. God literally had to rip Himself in two. The greatest sacrifice was God's. That is why John 3:16 says God so loved the world He gave. It was nothing easy for God. God literally turned His back on His Son to turn His face to you. It is like taking out

His heart and ripping it in two so we could enter in His love.

If God was willing to do this for you; if love split itself in two to embrace you; if Jesus went through so much for you, do you believe it can be ok to make an excuse and reject a sacrifice like this. What circumstance could there be in your life that could cause you to reject a sacrifice like this or even to put it off? What could make anyone want to extend His pain for another minute? *I would then address the reality of their spiritual state and the barriers they may have to accepting Christ.*

Life is real and the devil has many of us so messed up and backed into a corner that we cannot see how to accept Christ if we wanted. We are locked into some life situation that makes accepting Christ a contradiction. If this is your situation, this is what Jesus battled with in the garden. He was locked in a love relationship with His Father, there was no easy way to become sin. He eventually decided it was too much for Him, but said to the Father, "Not My will but Yours."

You may be locked into such a relationship with sin that you cannot see how you can possibly accept the love of the Father. The decision is the same, Lord I cannot do this on my own, I resign to your will. Take my like and complete the sacrifice. I will respond to you now. This is where faith is needed. It takes faith to accept Christ. Faith means it is impossible for you but if you believe God is able. If you had the answer for sin He would have had no cause to die. Let Him complete the process in your life by saying yes now. If you wait to do it on your own Satan will make it impossible. Like Jesus, we say to the Father, "Not my will but Yours. We surrender ourselves and leave it to Him to fix it."

Then make the altar call.

Would you like to give your life to Jesus now?

Will you be one of those who will say, I will not allow that kind of love and sacrifice to hurt for me any longer? Will you take your messed up life and by faith commit it all to Jesus Christ to work it out?

I am committed to praying for you and with you and watch God work the miracle of working it out for your good.

Most will say yes, they are ready to take the step of faith.

Lead them in the sinner's prayer

Give them assurance, that they are saved, in accordance with Romans 10:9-10. Encourage them to read the Bible; pray, get to a Bible-believing church.

Take their number and names. Some will be happy to give this.

Listen where they want to talk and take information to pray about.

Follow up. Pray for them daily and call them from time to time to encourage them and to find out about their walk. Mentor where applicable.

Follow up visits as part of mentorship.

THE MESSAGE IN THREE MINUTES

This message is a synopsis of the full message which you can use or variants of this where you realize there is no time.

Using Key Points Only

The Bible tell us that when Jesus was in the Garden of Gethsemene just before His crucifixion His sweat became as great drops of blood

What do you think caused that?

The pain of the cross was excruciating. He was mocked, abused. His back ripped in pieces; Nailed and hung by His weight on the cross. It could not be more excruciating, more torturous, more painful. Thinking about this could cause anyone to lose sleep.

But this was not the reason.

You see when Jesus went to the cross He took the sins of the whole world onto Himself.

He hated sin passionately. He had nothing to do with sin or the devil. The Bible says He was tempted as we are but never sinned. The thought of having our sin placed on him must have made His skin crawl; the thought of becoming sin must have made it rebel from the inside out.

It is like the most disgusting thing one could imagine. Like bathing in a cesspool or anything reprehensive.

To Jesus it was unimaginable. This must have caused the sweat

But that was not the only thing.

When Jesus took the sins of the world on Himself God had no option but to turn His back on Him, literally. That is why He cried out on the cross, "My God My God, why have you forsaken Me".

God has nothing to do with sin; if it is on kings, presidents; pastors; even on His Son.

It is not good enough to live a good life. If God turned His back on Jesus because of sin, He will not favor those who reject this great sacrifice.

Earning the wrath of the God He loved is something Jesus could not endure. He would always say I and my Father are one. I do nothing but what I see Him do.

He could not reconcile this. He could not come to terms with this. Everything else He could face, but not His Father hating Him; turning away. Not Love. It was mesmerizing. He sweated blood. It was so much He could do nothing but resign Himself to the heart of Love. Not my will but yours.

The sacrifice was as grueling in Heaven where Love had to watch His Son die; had to say no as He went through His most painful ordeal. Had to turn His back on love who did nothing deserving. This was very painful and heaven bled for Him. The heart of heaven was ripped apart. The greatest sacrifice was with the Father. Love had to literally rip Himself in two and turn away from Himself as something detestable in order to turn His face to you as someone He could enjoy. I am sure all the angels were in tears if they are allowed to cry.

This sacrifice tore heaven in two. God literally had to rip Himself in two. The greatest sacrifice was God's. That is why John 3:16 says God so loved the world He gave. It was nothing easy for God. God literally turned His back on His Son to turn His face to you. It is like taking out His heart and ripping it in two so we could enter in His love.

If God was willing to do this for you; if love split itself in two to embrace you; if Jesus went through so much for you, do you believe it can be ok to make an excuse and reject a sacrifice like this. What circumstance could there be in your life that could cause you to reject a sacrifice like this or even to put it off? What could make anyone want to extend His pain for another minute?
I would then address the reality of their spiritual state and the barriers they may have to accepting Christ.

Life is real and the devil has many of us so messed up and backed into a corner that we cannot see how to accept Christ if we wanted. We are locked into some life situation that makes accepting Christ a contradiction. If this is your situation, this is what Jesus battled with in the garden. He was locked in a love relationship with His Father, there was no easy way to become sin. He eventually decided it was too much for Him, but said to the Father, "Not My will but Yours."

You may be locked into such a relationship with sin that you cannot see how you can possibly accept the love of the Father. The decision is the same, Lord I cannot do this on my own, I resign to your will. Take my like and complete the sacrifice. I will respond to you now. This is where faith is needed. It takes faith to accept Christ. Faith means it is impossible for you but if you believe God is able. If you had the answer for sin He would have had no cause to die. Let Him complete the process in your life by saying yes now. If you wait to do it on your own Satan will make it impossible. Like Jesus we say to the Father, "Not my will but Yours. We surrender ourselves and leave it to Him to fix it."

Then make the altar call.

Would you like to give your life to Jesus now?

Will you be one of those who will say, I will not allow that kind of love and sacrifice to hurt for me any longer? Will you take your messed up life and by faith commit it all to Jesus Christ to work it out?

I am committed to praying for you and with you and watch God work the miracle of working it out for your good.

Most will say yes, they are ready to take the step of faith.

Lead them in the sinner's prayer

Give them assurance, that they are saved, in accordance with Romans 10:9-10. Encourage them to read the Bible; pray, get to a Bible-believing church.

Take their number and names. Some will be happy to give this.

Listen where they want to talk and take information to pray about.

Follow up. Pray for them daily and call them from time to time to encourage them and to find out about their walk. Mentor where applicable.

Follow up visits as part of mentorship.

CONCLUSION

RESPONSE TO THIS BOOK

THE EASE (E's) of ENGAGEMENT

ARE YOU IN THE GAME?

Can you see Jesus in the garden

Pouring out His heart and soul?

Can you feel the pain that cooked Him

As His blood ran red, not cold?

Would you have wiped the rain drops

Of exhaustion from His face

And hugged Him till He no longer

Felt that piercing pain?

That's the cry and pull of empathy

If you ever feel this way

His blood will not be wasted

You are in the game

When you read this book, could you feel the misery that Jesus must have felt when He took the sins of the world upon Himself?

If Yes, you have the first E: Empathy

The condemned, the hated innocent

Just pouring out His love

And the love that mocked and killed Him

Is killing Him right now

Will you cry to tell them stop it

It's too much for one to bear?

Or do you hurt Him as a habit

With sin and without care?

How does it feel to know some of the sins they brought Him misery was yours; the ones you have already committed and the ones you may still avoid?

If you are committed to value this sacrifice, take another E: Energy

To know sin separated

The Father and the Son
And to know Love remonstrated
When Love turned its back on Love
And the pain was elevated
Till it turned His sweat to blood
Was love being demonstrated
And you were the center of it all

It should spark enthusiasm
You refuse to hurt Him more
All the sin that was laid on Him
You refuse to add on more
Nor let the blood go wasted
Or offer nothing for His pain
From this moment on to love Him
Won't let Him die in vain

How does it feel to know the Father in heaven suffered such a painful conflict between Himself, having to turn away from His good Son because of no-good you, who has no good thing and can do no good thing living in your flesh? How does it feel to know God rejected Jesus in His most painful ordeal because He refused to omit you for His most pleasurable and satisfying relationship?

If you are energized to respond to this conflict of love, take another E: Enthusiasm

He hurts, you hurt

He is pained you agonize

To enter through love ripped in two

And to become love's winning prize

Committed to avenge Him

So it will not be tossed

Calvary to be continued

For you are living for the cross

Does it pain you to be the one to get between the Father and the Son; to see love ripped apart?

If you are empowered by this sacrifice, take another E: Engaged

Now let this be your anthem

Your confession every day
Your modus operandi
Now emphatically just say:

Satan thought He had Him
But as long as I am alive
I will live for all He died for
So His sweat will not be dried.
My heart, my soul, my energy
I will be put into the cross
With all in me to love Him
So He gets the final laugh

Do you believe it is appropriate for anyone to sit by and allow the sacrifice of Love and Jesus to be wasted? Have you put Satan to shame by accepting Jesus? Will you be so madly in love with God that you determine that this sacrifice will not go in vain while you are alive; while you breathe? Are you mad with the devil for what He caused heaven and Jesus to go through? Will you be one of those who will ensure Satan does not have the final laugh in the lives of the people this sacrifice was made for?

If you are animated and agitated for war, select the final two E's: Enraged and Emphatic.

If you have all the E's your life will never be the same, for nonchalance is buried by **empathy**, and understanding compels **energy** and **enthusiasm** that commit you, not just to words, but to action. You commit, your heart, your resources, your time, your strength and your mind to loving Him and responding to His heart poured out. Now commit yourself to be **engaged** with a passion that makes you so **enraged** with the devil that you stubbornly refuse to stand on the sidelines and watch Him win in the lives of people heaven suffered so much to liberate. It causes such a rush of adrenaline that compels you to be deliberate and **emphatic** about avenging the cross and the sacrifice the Father and the Son made that fateful day.

BONUS SCRIPTURES

FROM THE:

Caribbean Worship & Devotional Study

(CWDS) BIBLE

ISAIAH 53 – CWDS Bible

DESPISED and rejected,
Bruised, battered, grieved!
Wounded, chastised, dejected,
And He was not esteemed!
All we like sheep have gone astray,
Have turned everyone to his own way.
To bring us again, make us His sons,
He was despised, rejected,
Bruised, battered, grieved!

ISAIAH 53

1Who has believed our report;
oh, who has believed?
And to whom has the arm of the Lord been revealed?
2For He shall grow up before Him
as a plant tender and young,
green and freshly springing,
as a root out of dry ground.
He has no form or comeliness,
and when we look at Him,
there is no beauty that we should desire Him, *by His outward form.*
3He is despised and rejected of men;

a Man of sorrow and acquainted with grief;
and we hid, as it were, our faces from Him.
He was despised, and we did not esteem Him.
4Surely He has borne our griefs

and our sorrow He has carried.

We esteemed Him stricken,

smitten by God, and afflicted.

5For our transgressions He was wounded,

for our iniquities He was bruised.

He was chastised for our peace,

and by His stripes we were healed.

6All we like sheep have gone astray;

we have turned, everyone, to his own way,

and the Lord has laid on Him

the iniquity of us all.

7He was oppressed and He was afflicted,

yet He did not open His mouth to respond.

He was led like a lamb to the slaughter,

and as a sheep before his shearers is dumb,

He held His tongue.

8He was taken from prison and from judgment,

and who will declare His generation?

For He was cut off from the land of the living.

He was stricken for the transgressions of My people.

9With the wicked they made His grave;

but with the rich at His death,

for He had done no violence,

nor was any deceit in His mouth.

10Yet it pleased the Lord to bruise Him,

to put Him to grief as an offering.

When You make His soul an offering for sin,

then shall He see His offsprings.

He shall see His seed then and His days He will prolong.

The pleasure of the Lord will prosper in His hand.

11He will see the travail of His soul,

and He shall be satisfied.

By His knowledge, My righteous Servant shall justify many,

for he shall bear their iniquities.

12Therefore I will give Him a portion with the great.

He will divide the spoil with the strong,

because He poured out His soul unto death.

He was numbered with transgressors;

He bore the sins of many,

and for the transgressors He made intercession;

while He was despised, rejected; bruised, battered, grieved.

CWDS Bible Quotes

The arm of the Lord is powerful but the experience novel and progressive; He is a revelation that requires faith to fully process and experience.

The revealed arm of the Lord is not for those who receive the report but for those who believe it.

Beauty is defined by a heart of duty, not in how cute or socially cultured you are.

It must take sorrow to bear joy to the world for the devil does not give easy passage; it gives pleasure to those who bear sorrow to see their sacrifice received.

If sorrow is your name, then glory is your game; it took the Man of Sorrows to bring joy to the world.

The grief, the pain and the shame, was not His but ours; He bore it so we could experience His freedom and His joy.

The wounds of sin in all its depth opened the room of hope to escape from death.

The cross is a physical expression of the wounds Jesus receives every time we transgress.

Chastisement contrasts contentment and peace; He took the chastisement contending for your peace so you could take the peace and contentment even in the midst of conflict.

The sheep is cultured through sacrifice; it accepts the mind of its master and is led. Sacrifice is cultured by the sheep; it remains silent and submissive to the defense, vindication and will of its Master.

A sacrifice must be answered; the sacrifice of the innocent must be avenged by people incensed to ensure His death is not in vain, who are ready to live for what He died for; who will declare His generation?

The gravity of your accusation is not resolved in the purity of your innocence.

It does not matter how you die, who you die with or how you are buried; what matters is that you die for what you lived for, empty and fulfilled.

The pain of death is defeated by the pleasure of fulfillment; when sacrifice abounds to the blessing for others, when you see the fruit of your work, when the Lord is pleased with you, when you have a sure reward, no sacrifice is too great.

PRAYER POINTS

Mighty God, today I seek a new experience with You; greet my enemies with Your mighty arm. Amen.

I have received, and I have believed the report of the Lord; I speak to the hearts of unbelievers, 'Be tender to the wisdom of God's saving grace'. Amen.

Most High God, place the beauty of service and righteousness in my heart. Amen.

Man of Sorrows, I accept the joy You brought me through Your own sorrows; I reject all sorrows of the enemy but enter into Your sacrifice of joy. Amen.

My Jesus, my Lord; You were wounded for my transgressions; I consciously refuse to transgress so I do not reopen Your wounds. Amen.

PAIN, so much pain! Why should the innocent have to feel pain like this?

So much pain, as the whip pierced His back, taking blood, taking flesh!.....

The crowd cried, "Slay the innocent; the guilty release!"

Forgetting the healings and the bread they did eat.

Thorns were His crown as they mocked, bowing down;

The nails pierced His hands, as by His weight He was hanged.

Pain, so much pain, much more than one can say;

And the crowd, yes the crowd... they mocked Him all the way!

MARK 15

1Immediately, as morning came, the chief priests held a consultation with the elders, and with the scribes and the whole council.

They bound Jesus and carried Him away

and delivered Him to Pilate,

2and Pilate asked, "Are You the king of the Jews?"

He replied, "You rightly say so!"

3The chief priests accused Him of many things also, but He gave no answer to them.

4Pilate asked Him again, "Do You answer nothing? Do you hear how many things they accuse You of?"

5But Jesus gave no answer, so Pilate marveled at this.

6Now at the feast, they would let one prisoner go, whomever the multitude desired.

7And there was one named Barabbas who was bound with them; he had made insurrection against the crown.

And in the insurrection, he had committed murder also.

8The multitude cried aloud and desired Pilate to do the custom.

9Pilate answered, "Would you have me release the King of the Jews?"

10For he knew that for envy Jesus was delivered up by the chief priests.

11But the chief priests moved the people to ask for Barabbas' release.

12Pilate then asked them "What would you have me do, to Him whom you call King of the Jews?"

13"Crucify Him!" they cried out; "crucify that Man!"

14Then Pilate said to them, "Why, what evil has He done?"

O the great pain of that moment, for the answer was simply, none!

Guilty of death? No. Well... perhaps guilty of love!

And they cried exceedingly more, "Crucify Him!"

15And Pilate, willing to do so, to let the people contented go,

released Barabbas and delivered Jesus to be crucified, after

scourging Him.

The torturous whip brought excruciating pain,

as to be crucified, the soldiers led Him away.

16Into the hall called Praetorium they took Him, and they called

the whole band together;

"Into the hands of sinners...!" They gave the wounded and

hurting Man.

Now this was their time of play!

17They clothed Him with purple, so richly adorned;

in contrast they gave Him a crown of sharp thorns.

They platted it and placed it on His head **18**and saluted Him,

saying, "Hail, King of the Jews! Hail!"

19And they struck Him in His head.

"Hail, hail!" And with the reed they hit Him again and again!

Stabbed by the thorns, His back from stripes raw, and His head

prickly sore;

all in the house of His friends as at His heart they tore.

They spat on Him and mockingly worshipped Him on bended

knees;

20then they took off the purple robe, after their mocking ceased.

They put His own clothes back on and led Him away to be

crucified.

21And Simeon, a Cyrenian, who passed by out of the country,

the father of Rufus and Alexander;

they compelled to carry the cross.

22"They brought Him to Golgotha, which means, "The place of the skull."

23They offered Him wine with myrrh, but He received none.

24And when they had crucified Him, and parted His garments, they cast lots to decide which part each man should take.

25It was the third hour when He was crucified,

26and over Him, the accusation, "King of the Jews!" was superscripted.

27They crucified two thieves with Him, one on His left, the other on His right hand,

28and so was fulfilled the Scripture which said, "He was numbered with the transgressors!"

29Those who passed by railed at Him, wagging their heads and saying, "Ah, You who destroy the temple and rebuild it in three days,

30"now save Yourself. Come down from the cross!"

"Physician heal Yourself!" This between their teeth they tossed.

31Likewise the chief priests, mocking, said among themselves, "He saved others; He cannot save Himself.

32Let Christ the King of Israel now come down from the cross, that we may see and believe!"

And the thieves also reviled Him, *as He suffered pain for all of these.*

33Darkness was over the whole land, from the sixth hour to the ninth,

34and at the ninth hour, with a loud voice, Jesus cried,

"Eloi, Eloi, lama sabachthani," which, when interpreted means, "My God, My God, why have You forsaken Me?"

Jesus bore all the pain that before this He received;

but now, oh, no, not this, "My God, why have You forsaken Me?"

35And some that stood by, when they heard the sound, said, "He calls for Elijah!"

36And one went and brought a sponge and filled it with vinegar and placed it on a reed and gave Him to drink,

saying, "Let Him alone now; let us see whether Elijah will come and take Him down from the cross."

37And Jesus died, after He cried out aloud,

and the voice of His cry summed up His painful ordeal,

a throbbing persistent echo of pain as death brought Him relief!

38And from the top to the bottom, the veil of the temple was torn in two.

39When the centurion who stood beside Him saw He died after crying out,

he said, "Indeed, this was truly the Son of God!"

40There were also some women, looking on from far away:

Mary Magdalene and Mary, the mother of James the less, and Joses and Salome,

41who also followed Him and ministered to Him when He was in Galilee.

They had felt His every pain, as the moments dragged on torturously.

And many other women came with Him to Jerusalem.

42When evening came, because it was the preparation, that is, the day before Sabbath,

43Joseph of Arimathaea, a honorable counselor, who also waited on God's kingdom,

came to Pilate boldly and requested Jesus' body;

44and Pilate marveled asking if He was dead already.

45He gave Joseph the body, when the centurion affirmed His death.

46He bought fine linen and took Him down, and wrapped Him in it and laid Him in a sepulcher which was cut out of a rock.

He rolled a stone over the door, and so the sepulcher was sealed shut.

47Mary Magdalene and Mary the mother of Joses observed and saw the place where He was being laid.

As the quiet serene evening, calmly belied the traumatic, tumultuous and eternally significant pain-filled, punishing day!

CWDS Bible Quotes

They accused Him of many things among themselves but could find nothing; none of their witnesses agreed, yet they came accusing Him of many things before Pilate expecting Him to agree; He answered nothing.

Never be hung up on a moment, good or bad, be hung up on fulfillment, for moments will change and shift, but every changing moment must take you to fulfillment.

The same mouth to cry 'Hosanna' may be the same mouth to cry 'Away with Him! Crucify Him!' yet the same hands they pushed away and pierced are the same hands stretched out to heal them and to invite them into His kingdom.

It is demonic humor to see in every age the amazing things people trade the King and the kingdom for: death, depression, drugs, evil companions, sex, Barabbas and other murderers of their lives and of their destiny.

It is not the evil you have done that determines the evil they do to you, but the evil that is driving them and the envy in their hearts.

Injustice has the loudest voice and the lowest blows.

They did not ask for Him to be scourged but our sicknesses demanded it; Pilate obliged being caught up in a spiritual moment he could not understand or escape.

Mockery is the greatest expression of the devil's fear about you; mockery is the greatest confirmation of your spiritual truth; mockery is the purest reality of your destiny mocking the devil; mockery is an invitation to God to move on your behalf.

They commanded Simon to take up His cross by force; He compels us to take up our cross by love; yet He commanded us to take up our cross before He took to the cross Himself, for we are not taking upon ourselves His cross, we are taking ours in pursuit of Him.

So much time is spent by the religious dividing His garments and counting the spoils; we get lost in the economic reality for we miss the spiritual significance of the cross.

Jesus did not die in bad company, the robbers died in good company. It is very bad to be in the presence of the Lord Jesus, to experience His cross, to see His blood, and not encounter Him and change companies.

When envy has its day it will boil you in the fat of your goodness saying, "He saved others, now He cannot save Himself."

If you go down pulling others down you will have no help up or hope upwards; you will have sealed your fate down like the thief on the cross.

God has nothing to do with sin, even if it is on His own Son; He forsook His Son in sin.

There is none to do good as Jesus; if God forsook Jesus on the cross because of your sins, not His, how will He embrace you because of your goodness with you still clinging to the sins that He forsook His Son for?

The real sacrifice of Calvary was not the excruciating death on the cross, but Love turning its back on Love, the unthinkable; the separation of the Father and the Son, the inconceivable.

Women will always minister to men willing to selflessly minister; they will always gather to men willing to sacrifice. This is one for your marriage.

There are some who may not regard you in life but they will recognize and acknowledge you in death if you remain faithful.

God may not take you down from your cross but He will take the kingdom down to the people, and draw the people to your cross, because of the cross you bear.

Use your prominence to do something significant and of permanence for the body of Christ.

You may not have the privilege of the body of Jesus but you can lobby in the highest places for the body of Christ; you may not get the chance to host His body in your tomb but you can host the body of Christ which is alive in the earth today.

Stir up the boldness necessary to do what you need to do for the body of Christ even if it takes you out of your comfort zone.

His death on the cross brought eternity to time; the stone on His tomb sealed His body away in time, from time, but only for a time; the body of Christ was destined to rise and be dominant in the earth.

Mighty God, let every covetous spirit seeking a voice of accusation against the righteous receive angelic fire, in the name of Jesus.

I declare that I will fulfill my purpose, I will ride my devils to my destiny. Amen.

I will be like You my Lord Jesus, my hands are extended to my enemies, my love to those who hate me. Amen.

Jesus, I refuse to trade You for glut, greed, pleasure, pressure, pride or material things; I refuse to sell myself short. Amen.

I speak comfort and angelic defense to every believer kneeling at the sword of envy, in the name of Jesus.